THE PEEP OF DAY

The Peep of Day

Mrs F.L.Mortimer

Christian Focus Publications

© 2000 Christian Focus Publications

ISBN: 1-85792-585-8

This edition published in 2000
by
Christian Focus Publications Ltd.
Geanies House, Fearn, Ross-shire,
IV20 1TW, Scotland, Great Britain.
(www.christianfocus.com ~ email:info@christianfocus.com)

Cover design by Owen Daily

Printed and bound in Great Britain
by Cox and Wyman

PREFACE

Mrs Favell Lee Mortimer was born in 1802, the daughter of a London banker. She was religiously educated, and after her conversion at the age of 25, she threw herself with great enthusiasm into benevolent work. In particular, she was responsible for founding some parish schools on her father's estates, and was actively involved in their management.

At the age of 39 the author married Rev Thomas Mortimer, an Episcopal minister, but was widowed nine years later. After his death, she devoted her life to the care of the poor, and to writing books for the young. Her first great success was, "The Peep of Day," which passed through a great number of editions, and was translated into several languages. This was followed by further volumes, which included, "Line upon Line" in two parts. Her books made a lasting impact on the minds of the young in her day, and continue to influence generations long after her death in 1878.

In this edition of "The Peep of Day", every effort has been made to maintain as much of the original text as possible. It has been edited and adapted out of a desire to make it accessible to the contemporary reader whilst retaining the biblical accuracy and the author's ability to communicate with children.

Particular note should be taken of the new 'Suggestions for Study' which have been added to the start of each section and which include an activity which will involve the child in the next group of devotions.

Our hope is that this volume will be as much of a blessing in teaching today's generation as it was to previous ones.

Family Devotional Guide to the Bible

INTRODUCTION TO THE SERIES

The Family Devotional Guide to the Bible is made up of a series of six books which are excellent tools to use during your family devotional and worship times.

Although each book can be used on its own, the author's original intent was that they be used consecutively so that, starting with The Peep of Day, you and your children can go through the stories from the Bible together and discover the valuable lessons that can be learnt from them.

Using this series, you can progress from the story of Creation right through the Old Testament to the New Testament and the life, death and resurrection of the Lord Jesus Christ, the adventures and lessons of the Apostles and the early Christian Church.

All six books are an excellent family resource.

Family Devotional Guide to the Bible

BOOKS IN THE SERIES

1. The Peep of Day:
Lessons from both Old and New Testaments.

2. Line Upon Line I:
Lessons from Genesis, Exodus, Numbers and Joshua.

3. Line Upon Line II:
Lessons from 1st and 2nd Samuel, 1st and 2nd Kings, Daniel and Ezra.

4. Precept Upon Precept:
Lessons from the New Testament about the life, death and resurrection of Jesus Christ.

5. More About Jesus:
Further lessons from the New Testament about the life, death and resurrection of Jesus Christ.

6. Lines Left Out
Further Old Testament lessons not dealt with in The Peep of Day or Line Upon Line I and II.

USER'S INTRODUCTION

The aim of this book is to lead children to understand and to delight in the Scriptures.

If adults can meet with difficulties in the biblical text which commentaries will help them to overcome, children will obviously come across many more, some of which this book may help to clear up. Obviously the direction and teaching of a loving parent is the greatest help any child can have in understanding the Bible and its teaching, but this book and others in the series, will re-inforce that teaching and where parental guidance is not available this book will in some way help to fill that gap.

You should take particular note of the newly created 'Suggestions for Study' which have been added to the start of each section and which include an activity to involve your child in the next group of devotions.

Each chapter also contains a memory verse that relates in some way to the content of the chapter. Use these to encourage your child to commit these verses to memory as part of your study of the Bible.

In addition you will notice small numbers contained in the text of the chapters. These relate to notes provided at the end of each lesson, which you can use to encourage your child to get to know their way round their Bible by finding and reading the passages listed.

CONTENTS

SECTION 1
MY FAMILY AND ME

SECTION 2
ANGELS

SECTION 3
GOD'S WORLD

SECTION 4
JESUS HAS ARRIVED

SECTION 5
JESUS AT WORK

SECTION 6
THE LAST MEAL

SECTION 7
THE FINAL NIGHT

SECTION 8
JESUS DIES

SECTION 9
JESUS IS ALIVE

SECTION 10
THIS IS NOT THE END

SECTION 1

MY FAMILY AND ME

Introduction

In this section we will be learning about our relationships with our family, and of the way in which God created us as a special part of His creation.

Some Suggestions for Study

Make a family tree, including as many close relatives as you can. You might like to make it poster size and use photos or drawings of each family member. As you finish each lesson in this section, use your family tree as a guide in praying for family members.

LESSON 1
OF THE BODY

You have seen the sun in the sky.
Who put the sun in the sky? - God.
Can you reach up so high? - No.
Who holds up the sun that it does not fall?[1] - God.
God lives in heaven; heaven is much higher than the sun.[2]
Can you see God? - No.
Yet He can see you for God sees everything.[3]

God made everything at first, and God takes care of everything.[4] God made you, my child, and God takes care of you always.[5] You have a body; from your head down to your feet I call your body. Put your hand before your mouth. What do you feel coming out of your mouth?

It is your breath. You breathe every moment. When you are asleep you breathe. You cannot help breathing. But who gives you breath?[6] God does everything. God gave you this body, and He makes it live, and move, and breathe. There are bones in your body. God has made them strong and hard.[7]

There are some bones for your arms, and some bones for your legs. There is a bone for your back, and more bones for your sides. God has covered your bones with flesh. Your flesh is soft and warm.

In your flesh there is blood. God has put skin outside,[8] and it covers your flesh and blood like a coat. Now, all these things, the bones, and flesh, and blood, and skin, are called your body. It was kind of God to give you a body.[9] I hope that your body will not get hurt.

Will your bones break? - Yes, they would if you were to fall down from a high place, or if a car were to go over them.

If you were to be very sick your flesh would waste away, and you would have scarcely anything left but skin and bones.

Did you ever see a child who had been sick a very long while?

I have seen a sick baby. It did not have round cheeks like yours. The baby's flesh was almost gone, and its little bones were only covered with skin.

God has kept you strong and well.

How easy it would be to hurt your body!

If it were to fall into the fire it would be burned up. If hot water were thrown upon it, it would be scalded. If it were to fall into deep water, and not be taken out very soon, it would be drowned. If a great knife were run through your body, the blood would come out. If a great box were to fall on your head, it would be crushed. If you were to fall out of the window, your neck would be broken. If you did not eat some food for a few days, your body would be very sick, your breath would stop, and you would grow cold, and you would soon be dead.

You can see that you have a very weak body.[10]

Can you keep your own body from being sick, and from getting hurt?

You should try not to hurt yourself, but God only can keep your body from all harm, from fire and water, from wounds and bruises, and all kinds of sickness.[11] Kneel down and say to God, "Please keep my body from getting hurt." God will hear you, and go on taking care of you.

Questions for Lesson 1

Why does the sun not fall from the sky?
What does God give you every moment?
What are the four things that are called your body?
How might your body be hurt?
Who can keep it from getting hurt?

Scripture Verse

All comes from God.
'...[God] giveth to all life, and breath, and all things.' (Acts 17:25).

Notes for Lesson 1

[1] Heb. 1:3.   [2] Eph. 4:10.   [3] Prov. 15:3.   [4] Ps. 36:6.
[5] Acts 17:28.   [6] Isa. 42:5.   [7] Job 10:11.   [8] Job 10:11.
[9] Ps. 139:14.   [10] Job 4:19.   [11] Ps. 121:7.

* * * * * * * * * *

LESSON 2
OF PARENTS' CARE

I have told you about your body. Was your body always as big as it is now?

No. It was once very small indeed.

What were you called when your body was very small? - A baby.

Now you can take care of yourself, but then you could take no care at all.

Can babies walk, or talk, or feed themselves, or dress themselves? - No.

But God sent you to people who took great care of you when you were a baby.

Who were they?

Your dear mother and father; they took care of you then. They held you in their arms, and fed you, and took you out in the air, and washed you, and dressed you.

Do you love your father and mother? - Yes.

I know you do. But who gave you a mother and father? It was God who sent you to them.

A little while ago you did not exist.[1] Then God made your little body, and he sent you to your parents, who loved you as soon as they saw you. It was God who made your parents love you so much,[2] and made them so kind to you.

Your parents dressed your body in neat clothes, and laid you in a cradle. When you cried they gave you food, and hushed you to sleep in their arms. They showed you pretty things to make you smile. They held you up, and showed you how to move your feet. They taught you to speak, and they often kissed you, and called you sweet names.

Are your father and mother kind to you still? - Yes, they are, though they are sometimes angry.

But they want you to be good; that is why they are sometimes angry. Your parents send you to school, and they give you supper when you get home. I know they will be kind to you as long as they live.

But remember who gave you these parents.

Can your parents keep you alive? - No.

They can feed you, but they cannot make your breath go on.

Can your heavenly Father die?

No, never.

Does he love you? - Yes.

Even if your earthly mother and/or father are not good to

you, your heavenly father will always care for you.[3] He is always thinking of you. He is always looking at you. He gives you part of His things. He would like you to come and live with Him in heaven some day.[4]

God thinks of you every moment.[5] If he were to forget you, your breath would stop.

Do you ever thank your parents for their kindness? - Yes. You often say, "Thank you," and sometimes you put your arms round them and say, "I love you very much!" Will you not thank God who gave you a mother and father who keep you alive? When you speak to God, then you should say, "O, God, how good you have been to me! I thank you and love you."

Would God hear your thanks? - Yes; God would hear and be pleased.[6]

Questions for Lesson 2

What was it your parents did for you when you were a baby?
Did your parents make you breathe, and keep you alive?
Why did God give you a mother and father?
What should you say to God for giving you parents?

Scripture Verse

We should thank God.
'O give thanks unto the LORD; for *he* is good....' - (Ps. 136:1).

Notes for Lesson 2

[1] Job 8:9.   [2] Compare with Dan. 1:9.
[3] Ps. 27:10.   [4] Compare with 1 Tim. 2:3,4.

[5] Luke 12:6,7.   [6] Ps. 69:30,31.

LESSON 3

OF THE SOUL

Has God been kind to dogs?

Has he given them bodies? - Yes.

Have they bones, and flesh, and blood, and skin? - Yes.

The dog has a body as well as you. Is the dog's body like yours? - No.

How many legs have you got? - Two.

How many legs has a dog? - Four.

Have you got arms? - Yes; two.

Have dogs got arms? - No; it has got no arms, nor hands. But the dog has legs instead. Your skin is smooth, but the dog is covered with hair.

Is the cat's body like yours? - No; it is covered with fur.

Is the chicken's body like yours? How many legs has the chicken? - Two.

And so have you. But are its legs like yours? - No; the chicken has very thin, dark legs, and it has claws instead of feet.

Have you feathers on your skin? Have you wings? Is your mouth like a chicken's beak? Has the chicken any teeth? - No; the chicken's body is not at all like yours. Yet the chicken has a body - for it has flesh, and bones, and blood, and skin.

Has a fly got a body? - Yes; it has a black body, and six black legs, and two wings like glass. Its body is not at all like yours.

Who gave bodies to dogs, horses, chickens, and flies?

Who keeps them alive? God thinks of all these creatures every moment.[1]

Can a dog thank God?

No; dogs and horses, sheep and cows, cannot thank God.

Why can't they thank God?

Is it because they cannot talk?

That is not the reason.

The reason is, they cannot think of God. They never heard of God. They cannot understand about God.[2]

Why not? - Because they have no souls, or spirits, like yours.

Have you got a soul? - Yes, in your body there is a soul which will never die. Your soul can think of God.

When God made your body, He put your soul inside. Are you glad of that? When God made the dogs, He put no soul like yours inside their bodies, and they cannot think of God.

Can I see your soul? - No; I cannot see it. No one can see it but God.[3] He knows what you are thinking of now.

Which is the best, your soul or your body? - Your soul the best. Why? Because your body can die, but your soul cannot die.[4]

Shall I tell you what your body is made of? - Of dust. God made the dust into flesh and blood.

What is your soul made of?

Your soul, or spirit, is made of the breath of God.[5]

That little dog will die some day. Its body will be thrown away.[6] The dog will be quite gone when its body is dead. But when your body dies, your soul will be alive, and you will not be quite gone.[7]

Where would you be put if you were dead? - Your body would be put into a hole in the ground, but your soul would not be in the hole.[8]

Even a baby has a soul, or a spirit.

One day I saw a man carrying a box. Some people were walking behind crying. There was a dead baby in the box. - Was the soul of the baby in the box?

No; its soul had gone up to God.[9]

Will you not thank God for giving you a spirit? Will you not ask Him to take your spirit to live with Him when your body dies?[10]

Say to God, "Please, take my spirit to live with you when my body dies and turns into dust."

What is that part which can't decay?

It is your soul.

Your body will decay; it will turn into dust; but your soul will live for ever; it will never decay.

Questions for Lesson 4

What other things have bodies, as well as you?
Are their bodies like yours?
What have you besides a body?
Is your soul better than your body? Why?
What is your body made of? What is your soul made of?
Where will your body be put when you die?
Where do you hope that your soul will go?

Scripture Verse

What becomes of us when we die?
'Then shall the dust return to the earth as it was: and the spirit shall return unto God who gave it.' - (Eccles.12:7).

Notes for Lesson 4

[1] Luke 12:6.   [2] Ps. 32:9.   [3] 1 Kings 8:39.   [4] Matt. 16:26.
[5] Gen. 2:7.   [6] Ps. 49:20.   [7] Eccles. 3:21.   [8] Eccles. 12:7.
[9] 2 Sam. 12:23.   [10] 2 Cor. 5:8.

SECTION 2

ANGELS

Introduction
In this section we read that God created other beings called angels. We will learn that some are good and are there to help us, but others have rebelled against God and are intent on evil.

Some Suggestions for Study
Before each lesson think of some famous films or stories that have fantastic creatures in them. Write down their names or find pictures of some of them. Some of these creatures will probably be imaginary, that means that they aren't real. But God's angels aren't imaginary. They are real beings made by God.

Thank God for the power of our imaginations but also thank him that he is more amazing and more wonderful than anything we can imagine. Thank God for the angels he sends to guard us and pray that we may resist evil.

LESSON 5
OF THE GOOD ANGELS

You know that God lives in heaven. He has no body, for He is a spirit.[1]

Does He live in heaven alone? - No; angels stand all round His throne.[2]

What are angels?

Angels are spirits.[3] They are bright like the sun,[4] but they are not so bright as God, for He is brighter than the sun.[5] The angels are always looking at God,[6] and it is God that makes them shine so bright.

They sing sweet songs about God.[7] They say, "How good God is! How wise! How great!"

There is no night in heaven,[8] for the angels are never tired of singing, and they never wish to sleep.[9]

They are never sick and they will never die.

They never cry; there are no tears upon their cheeks, only sweet smiles, because angels are always happy.[10]

If the angels were naughty, they would be unhappy. Naughtiness always makes people unhappy.

The angels are good.[11] They love God very much, and obey all He says.[12]

They have wings,[13] and can fly very quickly.[14] God sends them down here to take care of us.[15] As soon as God tells an angel to go, he begins to fly.[16] They are very strong, and can keep us from harm.[17]

Would you like the angels to be near you at night? Do you know this verse or hymn?

I lay my body down to sleep,
Let angels guard my head,
And through the hours of darkness keep
Their watch around my bed.

You must ask God to send the angels, for they never go, except when God sends them.[18]

They do not have two fathers, as you have. The angels are the children of God, and live in God's house in heaven. When you do what your father tells you, then you are like the angels who obey God.

The angels love us very much. They wish we would grow up grow up to be good, and to come to live with them in heaven.[19] When a child is sorry for its naughtiness and prays to God to forgive him, the angels are very pleased.[20]

When a little child who loves God falls sick, and is going to die, God says to the angels, "Go and fetch that little child's soul up to heaven".[21] Then the angels fly down, the little darling shuts his eyes, it lays its head on his mother's bosom, his breath stops - the child is dead. Where is his soul? The angels are carrying it up to heaven.

How happy the child is now! His pain is over; he has become good;[22] he is bright like an angel.[23] His little body is put into a grave, and turns to dust. One day God will make his body alive again.

Will you pray to God to send His angels to come for your soul when you die?

Questions for Lesson 5

Who live with God in heaven?
What are the angels always doing?
Why are they always happy?

Why do angels come down here?

What is it the angels do for children who love God, when they die?

Can you make yourself good?

Scripture Verse

God bids his angels take care of us.

'For he shall give his angels charge over thee, to keep thee in all thy ways.' - (Ps. 91:11).

Notes for Lesson 5

[1] John 4:24.   [2] Rev. 7:11.   [3] Ps. 104:4.

[4] Matt. 28:3.   [5] Acts 26:13.   [6] Matt. 18:10.

[7] Rev. 5:11-13.   [8] Rev. 22:5.

[9] Rev. 4:8; Ps. 103:20.   [10] Rev. 21:4; Luke 20:35,36.

[11] 2 Pet. 2:4.   [12] Ps. 103:21.   [13] Isa. 6:2.

[14] Dan. 9:21.   [15] Heb. 1:14.   [16] Ps. 103:20.

[17] Ps. 91:12.   [18] Matt. 26:53.   [19] Matt. 18:10.

[20] Luke 15:10.   [21] Luke 16:22.   [22] Heb. 12:23.

[23] Matt. 13:43.

* * * * * * * * * *

LESSON 6
OF THE WICKED ANGELS

When did God begin to live in heaven?

God always lived in heaven.[1]

Once there was no such little child as you, but there always was God.

Once there was no sun, but there was always God.

Once there were no angels,[2] but there was always God.

No one made God; God was the first of all things, and God made everything.

A very long while ago God made the angels. How many angels did He make?

No one could tell how many. There were more than could be counted.[3] They were all good and happy.

But some of the angels grew bad. They stopped loving God, and grew proud and disobedient.

Would God let them stay in heaven after they were bad?

No; He cast them out, and put them in chains and darkness.[4]

One of these bad angels was called Satan. He is the chief, or prince, of the bad angels. He is called the Devil.[5]

The devil is very wicked,[6] and hates God. He can never go back to heaven again,[7] but comes here where we live,[8] and he brings the other devils with him.[9]

We cannot see Satan, because he is a spirit, but he is always walking about, and trying to make people naughty.[10]

Satan loves mischief; he does not wish to be good. It pleases Satan to see people in pain and in tears;[11] but it pleases him the most to see them naughty, because then he thinks that they will come and live with him in his dark place. He wishes that there will be a lot of people in hell, so he tries to make us do wicked things, and to keep us from praying to God.[12]

I cannot tell you how bad Satan is. He is very cruel, for he likes to give pain.[13] He is a liar, and teaches people to tell lies.[14] He is proud,[15] and wishes people to concentrate on him more than on God. He is envious, and cannot bear to see people happy.[16]

The devil hopes very much that you will come and live with him when you die. He knows that if you are bad like him, you will live with him. So he tries to make you like himself now.

When you are in a temper, or say, "I don't care," or when you are proud - that's what he is like.

Can God keep you from giving in to the devil an his evil ways? - Yes, He can; for God is a great deal stronger than Satan.[17] Besides this, God is always near you, for God is everywhere. Now Satan cannot be everywhere at the same time. It is true that Satan has a great many angels who go where he tells them; and that Satan and his angels come near you very often. But God is always with you; He is before you and behind you, and on every side of you; He is about your bed when you sleep, and about your path when you walk.[18] Therefore, you need not be afraid of Satan; only ask God to help you, and He will do so.

Satan is much stronger than you are;[19] but God is stronger than all. If anybody were to come to hurt you when you were alone, you would be frightened; but if you saw your father coming you would run to him, and you would not be frightened any more. Now God is our Father; He can keep Satan from hurting you. Pray to Him, and say, "O, dear Father, keep me from being wicked like the devil, and from going to hell."[20]

Questions for Lesson 6

Did the angels always live in heaven?
Who has always existed?
Why did God cast some of the angels out of heaven?
What is the name of the prince of the bad angels?
Why does Satan walk about here?
Can you keep yourself from Satan?

Scripture Verse

God punished the wicked angels.
'..God spared not the angels that sinned, but cast *them* down

to hell, and delivered *them* into chains of darkness....' - (2 Pet. 2:4).

Notes for Lesson 6

[1] Ps. 90:2. [2] Col. 1:16. [3] Heb. 12:22.
[4] Jude 6. [5] Rev. 12:9; Eph 2:2. [6] 1 John 3:8.
[7] Jude 6. [8] Job 1:7. [9] Rev. 12:9.
[10] Eph. 2:2.

[11] Ps. 35:15; Ps. 52:3; Ps. 109:17; All that is said of the wicked applies in a higher degree to Satan, as the author of sin; for Christ said to the wicked, 'Ye are of your father the devil, and the *lusts of your father* ye will do - (John 8:44).

[12] Luke 22:31; 2 Cor. 4:3,4. [13] 1 Pet. 5:8; Eph. 6:16.
[14] John 8:44. [15] Matt. 4:9.

[16] This is proved by Satan having ruined man, and by his continuing to tempt him.

[17] Ps. 89:8. - *To Teachers:* A very young child would not understand the remainder of this chapter, except the last sentence; therefore, it would be better to miss this passage, when the pupil is of a very young age.

[18] Ps. 139:3,5. [19] Eph. 6:12. [20] James 4:7

SECTION 3

GOD'S WORLD

Introduction

In this section, we will be looking at God as the creator of the world and all that is in it. We will learn that although God made men and women special, our disobedience brought suffering and death to the human race. We will see that God made a plan to save people from their rebellion and bring them back to him through Jesus.

Some Suggestions for Study

Find some old magazines, calendars or posters and look for pictures of people, places, animals, nature, space, stars etc. Ask each person to cut out one or two pictures after each lesson, and stick them onto a large piece of paper or card. Then use the collage as a visual aid for prayer and praise.

LESSON 7
THE WORLD - PART 1.
Gen. 1:1 - 10.

This large place we live in is called the world.

It is very beautiful. If we look up we see the blue sky; if we look down we see the green grass.

The sky is like a curtain spread over our heads, the grass like a carpet under our feet, and the bright sun is like a candle to give us light. It was very kind of God to make such a beautiful world, and let us live in it.

God was in heaven, and all His bright angels around Him, when He began to make the world.[1] God's Son was with Him - for God always had a Son,[2] just like Himself.[3]

His Son's name is Jesus Christ. He is as good and great as God, His Father. The Father and the Son are God: they always lived together, and they love each other very much.[4] The Father and the Son are one God, and they made the world.[5]

How did God make the world? - By speaking. First of all, God made the light. God said, "Let there be light," and there was light. No one can make things by speaking but God; God made things of nothing. He only spoke, and the light came.[6]

Then God made the air. You cannot see the air, but you can feel it. The air is everywhere. You can sometimes hear the noise it makes, for you hear the wind blow, and the wind is air.

Next God put some water up very high. The clouds are full of water; and sometimes the water comes down, and we call it rain.

God made a large, deep place, and filled it with water. God spoke to the water, and it rushed into the deep place. God called this water the sea.[7]

The sea is huge, and it is always surging up and down; but it cannot get out of the place in which God has put it; for God said, "Stay there."[8]

When the wind blows hard, the sea makes a loud noise, and roars.

God made some dry land for us to walk upon: we call it ground. We could not walk upon the sea nor build houses on the sea; but the ground is hard, and firm, and dry.

Now I have told you of five things that God made: the light, the air, the clouds, the sea and the dry land.

Let us praise God for making such a large and beautiful world.

Questions for Lesson 7

What is this place that we live in called?
Who was always in heaven with God?
Is Jesus Christ the same as God?
How did God make this world?
What was the first thing that God made?
What is it that you can feel, but cannot see?
What is the water in the sky called?
What is the name of the large deep place full of water?
What do we walk upon?
What are the first five things that God made?

Scripture Verse

How the light was made.
'And God said, Let there be light: and there was light.' - (Gen. 1:3).

Notes for Lesson 7
[1.] Job 38:4,7.   [2.] Prov. 8:23,29,30.   [3.] Heb. 1:3.
[4.] Prov. 8:30; John 14:31.   [5.] John 1:1,3.   [6.] Heb. 11:3.

7. Ps. 104:6-8.   8. Job. 38:10,11.

LESSON 8
THE WORLD - PART 2
Gen. 1:11-19.

When God made the dry land, there was nothing on it; it was bare. So God spoke, and things grew out of the ground.

Trees came out of it; they were covered with green leaves of different shapes. Some were called oak-trees, and some were called elm-trees, and some beech-trees. And some trees bore nice fruit, such as plum-trees, apple-trees, orange-trees, and fig-trees.

Vegetables grew out of the earth; potatoes and beans, cabbages and lettuces, they are called vegetables.

Corn came out of it. Some corn is called wheat, and some corn is called barley, and some is called oats. The ears of corn bend down when they are ripe, and look yellow like gold.

God made the soft green grass to spring up, and flowers to grow among the grass; flowers of all colours, and of the sweetest smell. The yellow buttercup, the white lily, the blue violet, and the rose, the most beautiful of all flowers.

I have told you of five things that grow out of the earth: trees, vegetables, corn, grass and flowers.

The world looked very beautiful when it was covered with grass and trees. But only God and the angels saw its beauty.

Afterwards God placed the sun in the sky, and made it shine all day and go from one end of the world to the other.[1] God made the moon to shine at night, and he covered the sky with stars. You never saw anything so bright as the sun. It is very large indeed, only it looks small, because it is a great way off. It cannot fall, for God holds it up.[2] God makes it move across the sky.

The moon does not shine as brightly as the sun, for God lets it be dark at night, that we may rest, and sleep soundly.[3]

Who could count the stars? - No one but God.[4] He knows their names and their number, too.[5] When we look at the moon and stars, let us think "How great God is! Yet He cares for the little birds, and loves the little children."[6]

Questions for Lesson 8

How many different sorts of things grow out of the ground?
Tell me the names of some trees, of some vegetables, of some kinds of corn, of some flowers?
What bright things did God put in the sky?
How many stars are there?

Scripture Verse

How wise God is.
He telleth the number of the stars; he calleth them all by their names. - (Ps. 147:4).

Notes for Lesson 8

[1] Compare Job.38:12.   [2] See Heb. 1:3.   [3] Ps. 104:19,20,22.
[4] Jer. 33:22.   [5] Isa. 40:26.   [6] Psa. 8:3,4.

* * * * * * * * * *

LESSON 9
THE WORLD - PART 3
Gen. 1:20-25.

God had made a great many things; but none of these things were alive. At last He made some living things. He spoke, and the water was filled with fishes, more than could be counted.

Some were very small, and some were very large.[1] Have

you heard of the great whale? It is a fish as long as a church.[2] Fishes are cold, and they have no feet, and they cannot sing, nor speak.

God made some creatures, more beautiful than fish, to fly about in the air. The birds; they perched upon the trees, and sang among the branches.[3]

Birds have wings, and are covered with feathers of all colours. The robin has a red breast; the goldfinch has some yellow feathers; and the jay some blue ones; but the peacock has very beautiful feathers. It has a little tuft upon its head, and a long train that sweeps behind; sometimes it spreads out its feathers, and they look like a large fan. The thrush, the blackbird, and the linnet, can sing sweetly; but there is one bird that can sing more sweetly still - it is the nightingale. At night, when all the other birds have left off singing, the nightingale may be heard in the woods.

Some birds swim upon the water; such as geese, and ducks, and the beautiful swan, with its long neck and its feathers like the snow.

Some birds are very tall. The ostrich is as tall as a man. It cannot fly like other birds, but it can run very fast indeed.

The eagle builds its nest in a very high place.[4] Its wings are very strong, and it can fly as high as the clouds.[5]

Another birds is the dove. It cannot sing, but coos softly, as if it was sad.[6]

I cannot tell you the names of all the birds, but you can think of the names of some other kinds.

There are other kinds of living creatures, called insects. God made them come out of the earth, and not out of the water, like fishes. Insects are small, and creep upon the earth; such as ants. Some insects can fly also; such as bees and butterflies. The bee sucks the juice of flowers, and makes wax and honey.

How beautiful are the wings of the butterfly! They are covered with little feathers, too small to be seen.

All the insects were good and pretty when God made them.

At last God made the animals. They came out of the earth when God spoke. Animals walk upon the earth: most of them have four legs. You know the names of a great many of them - sheep and cows, dogs and cats. But there are many other types; the squirrel that jumps from branch to branch, the rabbit that lives in a hole under ground, and the goat that climbs the high hills; the stag with his beautiful horns, the lion with his yellow hair, the tiger whose skin is marked with stripes.

Now God had filled the world with living creatures, and they were all good; even lions and tigers were good and harmless. I have told you of four sorts of living creatures: fish, birds, insects and animals.

All these creatures have bodies, but they don't have souls like you. They can move and breathe. God feeds them every day, and keeps them alive.[7] The Lord is good to them all.

Questions for Lesson 9

How many sorts of livings things did God make?
Tell me the names of some fishes, of some birds, of some insects, of some animals?

Scripture Verse

God is kind to birds and animals.
'He giveth to the beast his food, and to the young ravens which cry.' - (Ps. 147:9).

Notes for Lesson 9

[1.] Ps. 104:25.
2. Some have been taken of 100 feet long and almost as much in circumference; though now, in consequence of the increased activity

of the fishery, whales seldom live long enough to attain their full growth. *Encyclopaedia Britannica* Art. 'Cetology.'

3. Ps. 104:12.   4. Job 39:27.   5. Isa. 40:31.
6. See Ezek. 7:16.   7. Ps. 104:27.

* * * * * * * * * *

LESSON 10
ADAM AND EVE
Gen. 1:26 to the end of chap. 2.

Now I will tell you of the last thing God made.

God took some of the dust of the ground, and made the body of a man; then He breathed on it, and gave it a soul; so the man could understand about God. Adam was quite good like God.[1] Adam loved God very much.

God put him in a very pretty garden, full of trees covered with fruit. This garden was called the garden of Eden. God showed Adam all the animals and birds, and let Adam give them what names he pleased. He said to Adam, " I give you all the fishes, and insects, and birds, and animals; you are their master." So Adam was king over all things on the earth.

God said to Adam, "You may eat of the fruit that grows on the trees in the garden." Still God did not let him be idle, but told him to take care of the garden. You see how very kind God was to Adam.

But Adam had no friend to be with him; for the animals and birds could not talk to Adam. Then God said He would make a woman to be a friend to Adam. So God made Adam fall fast asleep. God took a piece of bone and flesh out of his side, and made it into a woman. When Adam woke, he saw her. He knew that she was made of his flesh and bone, and he loved her very much. Her name was "woman," and afterwards her name was Eve.

You have heard of all the things God made. They were all beautiful; and all the living things were quite happy; there was no pain, and no sighing, and no sin in all the world.

God had been six days in making the world. And when He had finished it, He rested on the seventh day, and made no more things.

The angels saw the world that God had made; they were pleased, and sang a sweet song of praise to God.[2] Jesus Christ the Son of God was pleased, for He loved Adam and Eve.[3]

How did I know about the world being made? It is written in the Bible, which is God's own book.

Let us count over all the things that God made: light, air, clouds, sea, dry land, things that grow out of the earth, the sun, moon, and stars and living creatures.

Questions for Lesson 10

What was the last thing that God made?
How did God make Adam?
Where did God put Adam?
What did God give him?
Why did God make Eve?
How did He make her?
How many days was God in making the world?
Tell me the names of all the things God made?

Scripture verse

How beautiful the world was at first.
'And God saw everything that he had made, and, behold, it was very good.....' - (Gen. 1:31).

Notes for lesson 10
[1] Eccles. 7:29.   [2] Job. 38:4,7.   [3] Prov. 8:31.

LESSON 11
THE FIRST SIN
Gen. 3.

Adam and Eve were very happy in the Garden of Eden. They talked to each other, and walked together, and they never quarrelled, and they praised God for all His kindness to them.

God used to talk with them sometimes. They were pleased to hear His voice, for they were not afraid of Him.

There was one thing that God had told them not to do.

There was a tree in the middle of the garden. Some beautiful fruit grew upon it; but God said to Adam and Eve, "You must not eat of the fruit of that tree; for if you eat of it, you will die."

Adam and Eve liked to obey God, and they did not wish to eat of this fruit.

You know that the wicked angel, Satan, hates God, and he hated Adam and Eve.[1] He wished to make them naughty, so that they would go to hell and be burned in the fire. So he thought he would ask them to eat that fruit. He went in to the garden, and looked like a serpent.[2]

He saw Eve alone near the tree.

He said to her, "Why do you not eat this fruit."

Eve answered, "No, I will not; we must not eat that fruit. If we do, God has said we shall die."

Then the serpent said, "You will not die; the fruit will make you wise."

Eve looked at the fruit, and thought it seemed nice and pretty, and she picked some and ate it; and she gave some to Adam, and he ate it.

It was very wicked of them to eat this fruit. Now they grew naughty, and did not love God.[3]

Soon they heard God speaking in the garden; then they were frightened, and they went and hid themselves among the trees. But God saw them; for He can see everywhere.

So God said, "Adam, where are you?" Then Adam and Eve came from under the trees.

God said to Adam, "Have you eaten the fruit that I told you not to eat?"

And Adam said, "It was this woman who asked me to eat some."

And God said to Eve, "What have you done?"

And Eve said, "The serpent asked me to eat."

God was very angry with the serpent, and said he should be punished for ever and ever.[4] God said to Adam and Eve, "You shall die. I made your bodies of dust, and they will turn to dust again."

God would not let them stay in the sweet garden. He made them go out. He would not let them come back. He told one of His bright angels to stand before the gate with a sword of fire, and to keep Adam and Eve out of the garden.

Questions for Lesson 11

What did God tell Adam and Eve not to do?

Who asked Eve to eat the fruit?

Why did he ask her?

What lie did the serpent tell to Eve?

Were Adam and Eve good after they had eaten the fruit?

Why did they hide themselves under the trees?

How did God say Adam and Eve should be punished?

Who drove them out of the garden?

Scripture Verse

How sin came into the world.

'...by one man sin entered into the world...' - (Rom. 5:12).

Notes for Lesson 11

[1] See 1 John 3:8.   [2] Rev. 12:9.   [3] Rom. 5:19.
[4] Gen. 3:15.

* * * * * * * * * *

LESSON 12
THE SON OF GOD
Gen. 3:14 - 24.

Are you not very sorry to hear that Adam and Eve were turned out of the garden?

It was not so pleasant outside of the garden. A great many weeds and thistles grew outside; but in the garden there were only pretty flowers and sweet fruits.

Adam was forced to dig the ground till he was hot and tired, for he could not always find fruit upon the trees.

Now Adam felt pain in his body sometimes; and his hair became grey, and at last he became quite old.

Eve was often sick and weak, and tears ran down her cheeks.

Poor Adam and Eve! If you had obeyed God you would have been happy for ever.

Adam and Eve knew that they must die at last. God gave them some little children; and Adam and Eve knew that their children must die too. God had told them that their bodies were made of dust, and that they must turn to dust again.

But there was something more sad still. They had grown wicked. They did not love praising God, as they once had done, and they liked doing many naughty things.[1]

They had grown like Satan; so Satan hoped that when their bodies were put into the ground their spirits would be with him, for Satan knew that the wicked could not live with God in heaven.[2]

And they would have gone to hell, and all their children too, had not God taken pity upon them. God, who is very kind, had found out a way to save them.

God had said to His Son, a long, long while before, "Adam and Eve and all their children must go to hell for their wickedness unless you die instead of them.[3] My beloved Son, I will send you; you shall have a body; you shall go and live in the world, and you shall obey Me, and you shall die for Adam and his children."[4]

The Son said to His Father, "I will come; I will do all that you desire Me to do. It is My delight to obey you."[5]

So the Son promised that He would die for Adam and Eve, and for their children.

How kind it was of the Father to spare His dear Son, whom He loved so very much![6] How kind it was of the Son to leave His throne of light, His bright angels, and His dear Father, and to take a body and to die![7]

You know that we are some of Adam's children's children. Jesus came to die for us. We are wicked, and we would go to hell, if Jesus had not promised to die for us.[8] We ought to love the Father and the Son, because they had pity on us.

Let us praise God with the angels,[9] and say -

"We thank You, O Father, for Your tender love, in giving Your only Son.

"We thank You, O Son, for Your tender love, in coming down to bleed and die."

The Father waited a long time before he sent His Son down to be a man.

All the time the Son waited in heaven he thought of what He had promised to do:[10] but He would not go and be a man till His Father pleased to send Him.[11]

Questions for Lesson 12

Were Adam and Eve happy after they had eaten the fruit?
Why not?
Who took pity upon them?
What did God desire His Son to do for Adam?
What did God's only Son say to His Father, when He told Him
to be a man and die?
Are we some of Adam's children?
Did the Son of God die for *us?*
Where would we go when we died if Jesus had not died for
us?
Did Jesus come down into the world as *soon* as Adam had
grown wicked?
Did He wait a *long* time, or a *little* time?

Scripture Verse

Who sent us a Saviour.
'...the Father sent his Son to be the Saviour of the world.' - (1
John 4:14).

Notes for Lesson 12

[1.] Rom. 8:7.
[2.] Luke 22:31; The constant efforts of Satan to tempt man to commit
sin, show that he is aware of the destructive nature of sin; as it is
undeniable that he desires to destroy man.
[3.] 1 John 4:10; 1 Pet. 1:20.   [4.] John 15:10.   [5.] Ps. 40:7,8.
[6.] John 17:24.   [7.] John 17:5   [8.] 1 Cor. 15:22.
[9.] Rev. 5:11-13.
[10.] Visits of the Son of God to man, in anticipation of his sacrifice, are
recorded often in the Old Testament. His visit to Abraham (Gen. 18); to
Jacob (Gen. 32); to Moses in the bush (Exod. 3); to Joshua (Josh. 5); to
Isaiah (Isa. 6) compared with John 12:41.

The Son of God is obviously referred to in the following passage: 'He bare them, and carried them all the days of old' (Isa. 63:9).
[11.] Gal. 4:4.

SECTION 4

JESUS HAS ARRIVED

Introduction

Jesus is the fulfilment of God's promise and plan to save people from their sin. This section looks at how Jesus arrived in the world as a little baby, and how different people reacted.

Some Suggestions for Study

Consider some examples of the promises which we come across in our daily lives. You could include the promise on a bank note, a product guarantee, a price promise/pledge, marriage vows etc. Use the example as an illustration and contrast it with God's promise. Note that while these earthly promises are usually good, they can be broken or become worthless with time. Contrast this with God's promises, which are always reliable and will last forever and give thanks.

LESSON 13
THE VIRGIN MARY
Luke 1:26 - 55.

God told Adam and Eve that He would send His Son down to die for them. But Adam and Eve did not love God; for they had grown wicked.

Could God make them good?

Yes, He could; for there is the Holy Spirit in heaven, and the Holy Spirit could come into them and make them good.

You know, my little children, we are wicked, and God can make us good with His Holy Spirit. If God puts His Holy Spirit in us, we shall not go to hell and live with Satan[1]

I hope you will ask God to give you His Holy Spirit. Say to God, "O, give me Your Holy Spirit to make me good!"

Adam had a great many children and grandchildren, and they had more children; at last the world was full of people - more people than you could count.

After Adam and Eve had been dead a long while, and when the world was full of people, God sent his son down into the world.

But God chose that His Son should be a little baby at first - because everybody is a little baby at first.

God sent His Son to be the baby of a poor woman. This woman's name was Mary. Mary had no children. She was a good woman, and loved God. God's Holy Spirit was in her, and made her meek and gentle.

One day an angel came to her. When Mary saw the bright angel she was frightened; but the angel said, "Don't be afraid, Mary; God loves you. He will miraculously enable you to have a baby who will be called the Son of God. You shall call his name Jesus. He will come to save people from their sins."

Mary was very surprised at what the angel said. She thought she was not good enough to have such a baby as the Lord Jesus.

When the angel had gone back to heaven, Mary sang a sweet song of praise to God for His goodness. Mary said, "My soul praises God, and my spirit is glad because of my Saviour."

Mary called her baby her Saviour, for she knew that He would save her from hell.

Questions for Lesson 13.

Did Adam and Eve *know* that God would send His Son to die for them?
Could God make Adam and Eve good again?
How could they be made good?
What must you ask for, if you wish to be good?
When did God send His Son down into the world?
Whose little baby did God's Son choose to be?
Who told her she should have a little baby?
What name did the angel say she was to give her baby?
What did Mary do when the angel had gone back to heaven?

Scripture Verse

Why Christ came.
'...Christ Jesus came into the world to save sinners...' - (1 Tim. 1:15).

Notes for Lesson 13

[1.] 2 Thess. 2:13.

LESSON 14
THE BIRTH OF JESUS
Luke 2:1 - 7.

Mary had a husband called Joseph. He was a good man, and very kind to Mary.

Now, before Mary's baby was born, a great king said that everybody must have their names written down.[1] So Mary and Joseph left their house, and went on a long journey. At last they came to a town called Bethlehem.

It was night. Where could they sleep?

They went to an inn, and said, "Please let us in. We have come from far away."

But the master of the inn said, "I have no room in my inn for you."

What could poor Mary do? Must she sleep in the street?

Mary said she would sleep in the stable, if the master would let her. So Mary and Joseph went into the stable. There were cows and donkeys in the stable.

While Mary was in the stable. God sent her the little baby He had promised her. She knew he was the Son of God, though He looked like other little babies he was unaffected by sin.[2]

She wrapped Him in some long clothes, called swaddling clothes; but she had no cradle for Him to sleep in, and she could not lay Him on the ground, in case the animals should tread upon Him; so she put Him in the manger, and she sat by Him to take care of Him.

How dearly Mary loved this sweet baby!

Other babies have cradles and soft pillows, but Jesus lay in a manger.

Questions for Lesson 14.

What was the name of Mary's husband?

Why did Mary and Joseph go on a long journey?

What is the name of the town they came to?

Did they sleep in the inn at night? Why not?

Where did they sleep?

What baby was born while Mary was in the stable?

Did Mary know it was the Son of God?

Where did she lay her baby?

What did she wrap him in?

Did Jesus look like other babies?

Was His heart like other babies' hearts?

Scripture Verse

About Mary and the Lord Jesus.

'And she brought forth her first-born Son, and wrapped him in swaddling clothes, and laid him in a manger....' - (Luke 2:7).

Notes for Lesson 14

[1.] The word translated 'taxed' signifies 'enrolled.' A general census of the Roman Empire was made at this time.

[2.] Luke 1:35; Heb. 4:15.

* * * * * * * * * *

LESSON 15
THE SHEPHERDS.
Luke 2:8 - 20.

There were some fields near Bethlehem. On the night when Jesus was born, some shepherds were sitting by their sheep in those fields. Why did they sit up at night?

To keep their sheep from the wolves and lions which walk

about at night. There are no wolves and lions where we live, but near Bethlehem there were some.

These shepherds saw a great light. A beautiful angel came from heaven. The poor shepherds were afraid; but the angel said, "Fear not, I have sweet news to tell you. God has sent down His own Son from heaven to save you from hell. He is a baby now, lying in a manger. Go to Bethlehem, and you will find Him."

When the angel had finished speaking, hundreds and hundreds of bright angels filled the sky, and began singing and praising God for having sent His Son to save men.

At last the angels went back to heaven, and the shepherds were left alone.

Did they stay with their sheep?

No; they said, "Let us go and see the Son of God."

They ran to Bethlehem, and then to the stable of the inn. There was a baby lying in the manger; Mary and Joseph were sitting by. The shepherds said, "This is the Son of God. Angels have spoken to us to-night, and told us where to find Him."

All the people in Bethlehem were very surprised when the shepherds told them about the angels and the Son of God.

Questions for Lesson 15

Who were in the fields near Bethlehem the night Jesus was born?

Why did the shepherds sit up at night?

What did they see in the sky?

What did the angels tell them?

Who sang songs in the sky?

When the angels were gone, where did the shepherds go?

Did the shepherds tell people what they had seen?

Scripture Verse
What the shepherds did.
'And they came with haste, and found Mary, and Joseph, and the babe lying in a manger.' - (Luke 2:16).

* * * * * * * * * *

LESSON 16
THE WISE MEN
Matt. 2.

There were some wise and rich men. They lived far away from Bethlehem. They knew that God had sent His Son to be a baby; but they did not know where to find Him; so God put a beautiful star in the sky, and God made it move towards the place where Jesus was.

So the wise men left their houses, and set out on a long journey; but first they said; "Let us bring some presents for the Son of God, for He is a king."

They took some gold, and some sweet-smelling stuff to burn.

They looked at the star as they went.

At last it stopped over a house in Bethlehem.

The wise men were very glad indeed.

They longed to see the Son of God.

They went in, and there they saw Mary and her child Jesus; they fell down and began to praise Him, and to call Him the Son of God, and the King.

They took out their presents, and gave them to Him. Mary was poor; but now she had some money to buy things for her little baby.

Questions for Lesson 16

Who came from a great way off to see Jesus?
Who told them that God had sent His Son to be a baby?
How did they find the way to Bethlehem?
What did they bring with them?
Where did the star stop?
What did the wise men do when they saw Jesus?

Scripture Verse

The Great King.
'...God is the King of all the earth; sing ye praises...' - (Ps. 47:7).

* * * * * * * * * *

LESSON 17
KING HEROD
Matt. 2; Luke 2:51,52.

There was a very wicked king called Herod. He lived a little way from Bethlehem. He heard that a baby had been born in Bethlehem, and that some people said that the baby was a king.

Now Herod did not want another king around besides himself. Herod didn't even want the Son of God to be king.

So Herod said, "I will kill this baby that is called a king."

Herod knew that this baby was in Bethlehem; but there were many babies in Bethlehem, and Herod did not know which was the baby that was called a king.

Some people knew who it was; but they loved Jesus, and they would not tell Herod. A very wicked thought came into Herod's mind. He thought, "I will kill all the babies in Bethlehem." Do you think God would let Herod kill His Son?

No. God knew what Herod meant to do. God sent one of His angels to speak to Joseph when he was asleep.

The angel said, "A wicked king wants to kill the baby. Get up, Joseph; take Mary and the baby far away." So Joseph got up quickly; he took his donkey, he put Mary on it, and she held the baby. It was dark when they set off. Nobody saw them go.

The next morning some men came with swords. Herod had sent them. They had come to kill all the baby boys. They opened every door, and said, "Is there a baby boy here?" Then they snatched him from his mother, and killed him, and the poor mother cried bitterly. If you had walked down the streets, you would have heard nothing but women weeping and crying out, "My pretty baby is dead; I shall not see him any more!"

Did they kill Jesus?

No: He had gone far away. His Father, God, had sent Him away. Herod could not kill Him, for God would not let Him die so soon.

At last King Herod died. Then God sent an angel to speak to Joseph when he was asleep. The angel said, "Joseph, go back to your own country; Herod is dead."

So Joseph took the donkey, and Mary, and the child, Jesus, and they all came back to their own country.

Joseph was a carpenter. Jesus lived with Joseph and Mary, and did all that they asked of Him. He was a wise child, and loved to think of God. God His Father loved Him, and everybody loved Him, because He was so meek and kind. The older He grew, the more they loved Him.

Questions for Lesson 17

Who wanted to kill Jesus when He was a baby?
Were there many babies in Bethlehem?

Did King Herod know *which* baby was the Son of God?
Whom did Herod desire to be killed?
Did he kill Jesus?
Why not?
Who told Joseph to take Jesus far away?
Did Herod know that Jesus had gone away?
Did Herod think that he had killed Jesus?
Whom did Herod send to kill the babies in Bethlehem?
Did Jesus ever come back to His own country?
Who told Joseph to take Jesus back to His country?
Why might Jesus be taken back to His own country?
What was Joseph's trade?
Did the people love Jesus when he was a child?
Why did they love Him?

Scripture Verse

Who can always help us.
'My help cometh from the Lord, which made heaven and earth.'
- (Ps. 121:2).

SECTION 5

JESUS AT WORK

Introduction
In this section we will look at the work Jesus went about doing for the Father who sent him.

Some Suggestions for Study
At the end of each lesson in this section, draw a picture of something that you think is an important part of the story you have just studied. Write an observation or a prayer on your drawing, and keep it as part of a collection for this section.

LESSON 18
THE TEMPTATION
Matt. 4:1 - 11.

At last Jesus grew to be a man. He knew that He must go from place to place, and teach people about God.

But first He went into the wilderness by Himself. There, He had no house to sleep in, no friend to speak to, no food to eat. In the night it was cold, in the day very hot.

There were no men, but there were lions, wolves, and bears.[1] At night they roared and howled; but Jesus trusted in His Father.

He ate nothing for forty days and forty nights; God kept him alive. When Jesus was alone, He spoke in His heart to His dear Father.[2]

At last someone came and spoke to Him.

Who was it?

Not a man, not a bright angel, nor God; it was Satan. I do not know how he looked. He had come to tempt Jesus to disobey God His Father.

Satan knew that Jesus was hungry. He said to Him, "Turn these stones into bread!" but Jesus would not, for God had promised to feed Him Himself.

After that, Satan took Jesus to the top of a great building that was much higher than a church. It is dreadful to be on the top of a very high place; it makes one tremble to look down from the top.

Satan said to Jesus, "Throw yourself down from this place; your Father will send His angels to keep you from being hurt, for you know that He has promised to take care of you."

Would Jesus have done the right things if He had thrown Himself down? No; Jesus knew that His Father would be displeased if He threw Himself down; and Jesus always did the thing that pleased His Father.

Then Satan took Him to the top of a very high hill. He showed Him all the kingdoms of the world. He said, "Look at these fine things. I will give all their authority and splendour to you. You shall have all the world for your own; only kneel down and call me God."

But Jesus said, "I will pray to My Father, and not to you."

Jesus loved His Father better than all the things in the world.

Adam and Eve listened to Satan, and disobeyed God: but Jesus did all His Father had told him. Adam was disobedient - Jesus was obedient.

Then Satan went away; and angels came from heaven and fed Jesus.

Satan goes about, trying to make children naughty. A lion could only eat your body, but Satan wants to have your soul and body in hell. Satan hates you. He is your enemy. But God is stronger than Satan.[3] Say to God, "Keep me from disobeying You" and He will keep you.

Questions for Lesson 18

When Jesus grew up, where did He go by Himself?

Were there beasts in the wilderness?

How many days was Jesus there?

What did He eat?

Who came to Him at last?

Why did Satan come?

What did Satan ask Jesus to do first?

Why wouldn't Jesus turn the stones into bread?

What did Satan ask Jesus to do when he had taken Him to the top of a high building?

Why wouldn't Jesus throw Himself down?

What did Satan show Jesus from the top of a hill?

What did Satan say Jesus must do, if He would have all these fine things?

Would Jesus do this?

Who fed Jesus after Satan had gone away?

What harm does Satan want to do to children, and to all people?

Scripture Verse

The devil is cruel.

'...the devil, as a roaring lion, walketh about, seeking whom he may devour.' - (1 Pet. 5:8).

Notes for Lesson 18

[1.] Mark 1:13.   [2.] John 16:32.   [3.] 1 John 4:4.

* * * * * * * * * *

LESSON 19
THE TWELVE DISCIPLES
Mark 1:16 - 20.

When Jesus was a man, He began to teach people about His Father. Jesus used to preach.

Where did He preach?

Sometimes He preached to people in a place like a church; sometimes He preached in the fields; sometimes He sat on the top of a hill and preached; and sometimes he sat in a ship, and the people stood by the edge of the water to hear Him.

Jesus did not always live in the same place; He used to walk about from one place to another.

Did Jesus walk about alone? - No; He always had twelve friends with Him. He called them His twelve disciples. One was called Peter, and another John, and another James, and another Thomas. But I will not tell you the names of all, in case you forget them.

Peter was a fisherman. He had a little ship, and he used to catch fish in the day and in the night. James and John had another little ship, and they used to catch fish.

One day Jesus passed by their ships, and Jesus saw Peter and his brother Andrew throwing a net into the sea to catch fish, and Jesus said to them, "Come with Me." And Peter and Andrew left their nets, and their ships, and went with Jesus.

And Jesus went a little farther, and He saw James and John sitting in their ship, mending the holes in their nets, and Jesus said to them, "Come with Me"; and they left their nets, and went with Jesus.

Jesus called what people He pleased to come with Him.

Shall I tell you why Jesus chose to have twelve friends with Him? What do you think was the reason?

Jesus wished to teach them about God His Father,[1] that they might teach other people about Him.[2] They liked being with Him, and listening to His words.[3] Would you have liked to have been with Jesus?

When Jesus was alone with His disciples, He used to tell them secrets about God[4] and heaven. They loved Him very much indeed;[5] they called Him Master and Lord.[6] Jesus loved them still more than they loved Him,[7] and He called them His friends.[8]

Jesus used to give them part of His things. But Jesus had no house to live in,[9] and He had very little money.[10] Sometimes Jesus and His friends were very tired with walking far,[11] and sometimes they were very hungry and thirsty.[12] But kind people often asked them to come into their houses, and gave them food.[13] Other people laughed at Jesus, and called Him names.[14]

Were the disciples good? - They were bad, like us; but Jesus put His Spirit into them, and made them better.[15] The disciples were not as good as Jesus was; they often quarrelled with each other,[16] and sometimes they were unkind to poor people.[17]

Questions for Lesson 19

Where did Jesus preach?

How many disciples had Jesus?

Did they ever quarrel?

Can you tell me the names of some of them?

What was Peter doing when Jesus told him to come with Him?

What were James and John doing when Jesus called them?

Why did Jesus choose to always have some friends with Him?

What did they call Jesus?

What did He call them?

Did they love Jesus?

Why did they like being with Him?

Did Jesus give them money or fine things?

Why were the disciples good?

Scripture Verse

Christ was very poor.

'...Foxes have holes, and birds of the air have nests; but the Son of man hath no where to lay his head.' - (Luke 9:58).

Notes for Lesson 19

[1] John 17:6.   [2] Mark 3:14.   [3] John 6:67,68.
[4] Mark 4:34.   [5] John 16:27.   [6] John 13:13.
[7] John 15:9.   [8] John 15:15.   [9] Luke 9:58

[10] Jesus having recourse to a miracle to procure money to pay tribute, testifies to his poverty; and his sharing it with Peter ('Give them for me

and thee') shows that he shared his supplies with his disciples.' - (Matt. 17:24 -27).

11. John 4:6.   12. Matt. 12:1
13. Luke 10:38; John 12:2.   14. John 8:48.   15. John 15:3.
16. Luke 22:24.   17. Matt. 15:23.

* * * * * * * * * *

LESSON 20
THE FIRST MIRACLE
John 2:1 - 11.

I told you that some people used to ask Jesus to come into their houses. I will now tell you about a man who did ask Jesus. This man gave a feast, and Jesus came to the feast; Mary, Jesus' mother came; and the disciples came. There were a great many more people besides at the feast.

There was some wine for the people to drink; but there was so little, that very soon it was all gone.

Jesus knew that the wine was gone. Couldn't Jesus give the people more wine? - Yes; for He made the world and all things in it.

There were some large stone jars in the room. Jesus said to the servants, "Fill the jars with water," and they filled them quite full.

Then Jesus said, "Take some, and give it to the master to drink." The servants did so; but Jesus had turned the water into wine.

When the master had tasted it, he said, "What nice wine this is! Where did it come from?"

The servants told him how Jesus had told them to fill the jars with water. Then all the people at the feast knew that Jesus had turned the water into wine.

This was the first wonder that Jesus did; it was called a miracle.

Why did Jesus do miracles?

To show people that He was the Son of God.

The disciples were now sure that Jesus was the Son of God.

Questions for Lesson 20

When Jesus was at the feast, what did the people run out of?

How did Jesus make more wine?

What was the first miracle Jesus did?

Scripture Verse

What the Father gave to the Son.

'The Father loveth the Son, and hath given all things into his hand.' - (John 3:35).

* * * * * * * * * *

LESSON 21
SEVERAL MIRACLES
Luke 6, 7.

After Jesus had turned the water into wine, He did a great many wonders. He made blind people see, and deaf people hear, and dumb people speak, and lame people walk.

When Jesus came to a place, all the sick people crowded round Him.

Jesus did not send them away because they disturbed Him, but He cured them all - yes - every one.[1]

This was the way in which He cured one blind man. He said, "See!" and the man could see at that moment.[2]

This was the way in which He cured a man who was deaf

and could hardly speak. Jesus put his fingers into his ears, and touched his tongue, and looked up to His Father in heaven, and said, "Be opened!" The man's ears were opened, his tongue was lossened and he could speak plainly.[3]

Once Jesus saw a poor, sick man lying on a bed, and Jesus said to him, "Would you like to be made well?" The poor man said he wished very much to be made well. Then Jesus said, "Get up; carry your bed, and walk." The man tried to get up, and he found that he could; for Jesus gave him strength.[4]

One day Jesus was in a place like a church; He was preaching, when He saw a poor woman whose back was bent, so that she could not lift up her head. Jesus said, "Woman, I have made you well;" and then Jesus touched her with His hands, and her back grew straight, and she began to praise God.[5]

Sometimes Jesus made dead people alive again. That was more wonderful than making sick people well.

Once Jesus was walking on the road. A great many people were walking after Him, for people liked to see Him do wonders, and to hear Him talk. They met some men carrying a dead man to put him in the ground.

A poor old woman came after, crying very much. She was the mother of the dead man. He was her only son. Jesus was very sorry to see her cry. He came up to her and said, "Do not cry"; and then He touched the coffin. There was no top to it; the dead man was lying in it.

Jesus said, "Get up, young man!" He sat up and began to speak. Then Jesus said to his mother, "Here is your son."

All the people were surprised, and said, "This must be the Son of God. He can make dead people live again."

Questions for Lesson 21

Why did sick and blind people come to Jesus?

How did He cure one blind man?

How did He cure a deaf and dumb man?

What did He say to a man who was ill in bed?

What did He say to the woman whose back was bent?

What could Jesus do that was more wonderful than making sick people well?

When Jesus was walking along the road what did he see being carried by some men?

Who was crying very much because the man was dead?

What did Jesus say to the dead man?

What did the men do?

What did people say when they saw a dead man come to life?

Scripture Verse

The wonders that Jesus did.

'...[God] maketh both the deaf to hear, and the dumb to speak. - (Mark 7:37).

Notes for Lesson 21

1. Luke 4:40.　　　2. Luke 18:42.　　　3. Mark 7:32-35.
4. John 5:5 - 9.　　　5. Luke 13:11-13.

* * * * * * * * * *

LESSON 22
THE SINNER AND SIMON
Luke 7:36 to end.

Why did Jesus come into the world? To save us from hell.

But why did God say that people must go to hell? Because everybody was naughty.

Jesus can forgive people their naughtiness, and make them good. But Jesus will not forgive people who are not sorry. I will tell you of a proud man who was not sorry, and of a poor woman who was sorry.

A rich proud man asked Jesus to come and dine with him. Why did he ask Jesus? He did not love Him - he only asked Him so that he might hear Him talk; but Jesus said He would come.

The proud man treated Jesus very unkindly. He didn't welcome Jesus into his house as he should have.

A poor woman, who had been very naughty, saw Jesus go into the rich man's house. She came up behind Jesus, and began to cry for all her naughtiness. She knew Jesus could forgive her, and she loved Jesus.

She had brought a box of ointment with her; she stooped down, and her tears fell upon Jesus' feet, and with her tears she washed them; she wiped them with her long hair, and then poured the sweet ointment upon them, and kissed them.

The rich man looked at the woman very angrily; he knew she had been very naughty, and he was angry at seeing Jesus being so kind to her.

But Jesus said to the proud man, "This woman has been very naughty; but I have forgiven her, and she loves Me very much. She loves Me a great deal more than you do.

You gave me no water for My feet; but she has washed My feet with her tears. You gave Me no kiss; but she has kissed My feet ever since I came in. You gave Me no ointment; but she has poured sweet ointment upon My feet."

Then Jesus spoke kindly to the woman, and said to her, "Your sins are forgiven."

So Jesus comforted this poor woman, but the proud man and his friends grew still more angry.

Jesus will forgive your sins if you are sorry, and if you ask

Him;[1] but if you think yourself good, He will not forgive you; for Jesus cannot bear proud people.[2] Though you are but a little child, you have done a great many wrong things; and you do not deserve to go to heaven. Oh, I hope Jesus will forgive you! I hope the Holy Spirit will come into your heart, and make you feel very sorry for your sins. Then Jesus will forgive you, and you will love Him, as this poor woman did.

Questions for Lesson 22

How did the rich man behave towards Jesus, when he asked Him to eat with him?
What did the naughty woman do to Jesus?
Why did she love Jesus so very much?
Why did Jesus forgive her all her naughtiness?
Will Jesus forgive you your naughtiness, if you are sorry?

Scripture Verse

God is merciful.
'For thou, Lord, art good, and ready to forgive: and plenteous in mercy unto all them that call upon thee.' - (Ps. 86:5).

Notes for Lesson 22

[1] 1 John 1:9. [2] See the parable of the Pharisee/publican - (Luke 18).

* * * * * * * * * *

LESSON 23
THE STORM AT SEA
Luke 8:22 - 25.

Jesus often went into a ship with His disciples. Peter had a ship of his own, and John had another ship, and they liked to lend their ships to Jesus.

Once they were all in a ship, when the wind blew very hard and the water moved up and down, and came over the ship. The disciples were afraid that they would be drowned.

Jesus had fallen asleep, and was lying on a pillow. The noise of the wind and of the water had not awakened Him.

His disciples ran to Him, and cried, "O Master! Don't you care for us? Will you let us die?"

Then Jesus got up and said to the wind, "Wind, be still!" and He said to the water, "Be still!"

The wind left off blowing, and the water was smooth, and quiet.

Then Jesus said to His disciples, "Why were you afraid? Why didn't you believe that I would take care of you?"

Jesus knew that they were tossed about, and He would have kept them safe, even though He was asleep.

The disciples said one to another, "Jesus is the Son of God; even the wind and the waters obey Him."

Questions for Lesson 23

What made the disciples afraid, when they were in a ship?
Was it wrong of them to be afraid?
What did Jesus say to the wind and to the water?
What did the disciples say when they saw the wind and the water obey Jesus?

Scripture Verse

What the disciples said about Jesus after the storm.
'...for he [Jesus] commandeth even the winds and water, and they obey him...' - (Luke 8:25).

LESSON 24
JAIRUS' DAUGHTER.
Luke 8:41 to end.

A rich man came to Jesus, and fell down at His feet and said, "I have one little girl, and she is very sick; please come and make her well."

Jesus went with the rich man. When they were near the house some servants came out and said, "The little girl has just died; no one can make her well now."

But Jesus said, "Don't be afraid; I can make her well."

Jesus said to the father and mother of the little girl, "Come with Me into the house. Peter, James, and John, you may come in, but no one else."

So they went up into the room where the little girl was lying in bed. A great many people were in the room singing sad songs, and crying, because the child was dead. But Jesus said, "stop crying. The girl is only sleeping; she is not dead." Jesus said she was asleep, because He was about to bring her back to life again. But the people laughed at Jesus, and said, "She is dead"; and they would not believe that He could make her alive again.

Jesus said, "These people must leave the room." So He sent them out, and shut the door; but he let the father and mother, and Peter, and James, and John stay in the room. He took the little girl's hand, and said, "Arise!" and first she sat up, and then she got up out of bed, and walked about the room. She was twelve years old. Jesus then said, "Bring her something to eat."

The father and mother were very surprised at what had happened.

Questions for Lesson 24

Did Jesus ever make a dead child alive again?
Who were sitting round her bed when Jesus came?
Why did Jesus say that the girl was asleep?
What did Jesus do to the people who laughed at Him?
Who did Jesus allow to stay in the room?
How old was the girl?

Scripture Verse

God does everything.
'The Lord killeth and maketh alive: he bringeth down to the grave, and bringeth up.' - (1 Sam. 2:6).

* * * * * * * * * *

LESSON 25
THE LOAVES AND FISHES
Matt. 14:13 - 22.

Once Jesus went into the wilderness with His disciples, and a great many people came after Him; then Jesus preached to the people, and told them about His Father, and how He Himself had come down from heaven to save them from Satan. They listened to Him from morning till night.

When it was getting dark the disciples came to Jesus and said, "Won't you send the people home, for it is late?"

But Jesus knew that the people had had nothing to eat all day, and He did not like to send them home tired and hungry. So he said to his disciples, "Can't you feed them?"

"No," they said; "we have only five loaves and two small fishes, and see how many people there are!"

But Jesus said, "Make them sit down on the grass, and

bring the loaves and fishes to Me." So the disciples made them all sit down.

There were a great many people, as many as would fill ten churches - five thousand men, besides women and little children. How tired the little children must have been! It was time for them to have their supper and go to bed.

We shall hear how Jesus fed all these people.

They sat down on the green grass. Jesus took the loaves and fishes; first He lifted up His eyes to His Father, and thanked Him for the food, and then He took a piece of bread, and gave it to Peter, and said, "Feed all these people sitting there;" and He gave another piece to John, and said, "Feed these people;" and He gave a piece of bread and fish to each of the disciples, and told each to feed some people.

One little piece of bread would not be enough for all the children in this room; but Jesus made the bread enough for all the people. Everyone had enough, and they threw on to the grass a lots of little pieces. But Jesus said to His disciples, "Take some baskets, and pick up the crumbs;" and they filled twelve baskets full of little bits of bread. Then Jesus told the people to go home.

What a wonder Jesus had done! Yet you know that He feeds you, and all the people in the world.

How does He feed you? - He gives you bread.

What is bread made of? - flour.

What is flour made of? - corn.

Who makes corn? - God makes the corn.

What does He make it of? - nothing. God makes things out of nothing. Jesus is God, and makes the corn grow;[1] so you see that Jesus feeds you. If He did not make corn grow in the fields we would die. But He will not forget us. He even remembers the little birds. They can't plough or to sow corn, or to reap, or to put corn into barns, yet God does not let them starve.[2] The birds cry to God, and He hears them, and lets them find food.[3] Now God loves us much better than He loves the little birds, because we have souls; so He will certainly hear us when we pray to Him.

If you had no bread at home, and if you had no money to buy some, God would hear you, if you loved Him. He would not let you starve.[4] Won't you ask God for bread every day, and say, "Give me this day my daily bread?"

We ought to thank God for the food we eat; before we eat breakfast, or dinner, or supper, we should say, "I thank You, O Lord, for this nice food."

Questions for Lesson 25

Did any people come to hear Jesus preach?
Why didn't Jesus like to send them home at night?
How many loaves and fishes did Jesus feed them with?
Who gave the people the bread and fish?
Did the people leave any of the bread?
Where were the little pieces of bread put?
What does God make grow in the fields?
Would you get any bread if God did not make the corn grow?
Does God feed creatures besides men, women, and children?
Why does God take more care of you than of the birds?

Scripture Verse

The way in which God feeds men and beasts.
'He causeth the grass to grow for the cattle, and herb for the service of man; that he may bring forth food out of the earth.' - (Ps. 104:14).

* * * * * * * * * *

LESSON 26
THE KINDNESS OF JESUS
Matt. 15:21 - 28; Mark 10:13 - 16.

I told you that the disciples were sometimes unkind; but Jesus was always kind.

Once a poor woman came crying after Jesus, saying, "O Lord, I have a little daughter who is very sick." Jesus did not answer her at first, and the disciples were unkind, and wished her to be sent away. She cried so loud, they said to Jesus, "Send her away."

The poor woman fell down at Jesus' feet, and said, "Lord, help me!" And Jesus had pity on the woman, and said, "I will do what you wish."

The poor woman was glad to hear this, and she went home and found that her daughter was quite well.

Another time the disciples were unkind to some little children. Some poor women brought the children to Jesus, but the disciples would not let the women come near.

"Go away," they said; "you must not bring the babies here to trouble us."

But Jesus heard them speak, and was angry with the disciples. Jesus would not let the children go away. He said to the disciples, "Suffer them to come to Me: do not send them away."

Then He took the children in His arms, and put His hands upon them, and prayed to His Father, and blessed them.

O, happy little children, to be taken into Jesus' arms!

Jesus loves meek and gentle children. They are Jesus' lambs.[1] Jesus is their Shepherd, and He will take them to heaven when they die.

Questions for Lesson 26

Were the disciples as kind as Jesus?

How did they behave to a poor woman who wanted Jesus to help her?

What did they say to the poor women who brought their children to Jesus?

What did Jesus say to the disciples when they were sending the children away?

What did Jesus do to the children when they came to Him?

What sort of children does Jesus love?

Are there any children in heaven?

Scripture Verse

What Jesus said to his disciples when He called the children to Himself.

'But Jesus called them unto him, and said, Suffer little children to come unto me, and forbid them not; for of such is the kingdom of God.' - (Luke 18:16).

Notes for Lesson 26

[1.] Ezek. 34:31; Isa. 40:11.

LESSON 27
THE LORD'S PRAYER

When Jesus was in the world, He loved to think of His Father in heaven. He liked to be alone, that He might pray to His Father; sometimes the tears ran down His cheeks while He prayed.[1]

One night Jesus prayed all night alone upon the top of a high hill.[2]

Sometimes Jesus prayed to His Father while His disciples stood near and listened.

Once when Jesus had been praying with them they said, "Teach us to pray." Then Jesus taught them a little prayer.

It was this: "Our Father who is in heaven, hallowed be Your name. Your kingdom come. Your will be done on earth, as it is in heaven. Give us this day our daily bread. And forgive us our trespasses as we forgive them that trespass against us. And lead us not into temptation, but deliver us from evil; for Yours is the kingdom, and the power, and the glory, for ever and ever. Amen."[3]

I know that you say this prayer night and morning. Your mothers taught you to say it. But did you know who said it first? It was Jesus, the Lord; so it is called "The Lord's Prayer."

It is a very beautiful prayer, for Jesus said it; but it is hard for children to understand it.

What is the meaning of "Hallowed be Your name"?

Let God's name be praised.

What are "trespasses"?

Trespasses are sins.

Ask God to forgive your sins, or your trespasses.

Do you ever pray to God when you are alone?

You may pray to Him in any PLACE - in the house or in the garden.

You may pray to Him at any TIME - in the night or in the middle of the day.

You may ask Him for ANYTHING you want, just as you ask your father.[4]

What will you ask Him for? Will you ask Him to give you bread, and clothes, and a house to live in?

Yes, ask Him for these things, but most of all - ask Him for His Holy Spirit.

It is better to have the Holy Spirit than to have all the toys, all the money, all the flowers, all the birds, all the beautiful things in the world.

Why is it better?

Because the Holy Spirit will make you love God, as the angels do, and will make you live for ever and ever.

Will you say this little prayer to God? - "O, my Father, please give me Your Holy Spirit, for Christ's sake."

Questions for Lesson 27

Why did Jesus choose to be alone sometimes?

Did Jesus ever pray to His Father when His disciples were with Him?

What did they ask Jesus to teach them?

What prayer did Jesus teach them?

What is the meaning of "Hallowed be Your name"?

What is the meaning of "Trespass?"

What must you ask God for, to make you good?

Will God give you the Spirit if you ask Him?

Scripture Verse

When we should pray.

'Evening, and morning, and at noon, will I pray, and cry aloud: and he shall hear my voice.' - (Ps. 55:17).

<u>Notes for Lesson 27</u>

1. Heb. 5:7.   2. Luke 6:12.   3. Matt. 6:9-13
4. Luke 11:13.

* * * * * * * * * *

LESSON 28
JESUS FORETELLS HIS DEATH
Matt. 16:21 to end.

Jesus knew everything that would happen,[1] and He knew that He must soon die.

He used to tell His secrets to His disciples; so He took them into a place by themselves, and said, "I will soon leave you: the wicked people will take Me, and bind Me with ropes, and beat Me, and laugh at Me, and nail Me on a cross; but I shall soon be alive again."

The disciples could not bear to hear Jesus talk of dying, for they loved Him very much. They all looked very sad, and Peter said, "You shall not die;" but Jesus said, "I must die to save men, and to please My Father."

The Father had desired that Jesus should die, and He would not disobey His Father.[2]

Most of the people who wished to kill Jesus lived in a great town called Jerusalem. Jesus used to go to Jerusalem very often, and he used to preach there.

Why did some people hate Jesus? - Because He told them of their wickedness.[3]

He used to say to them, "You do not love God, who is My Father, but you are proud and vain.[4] You wish to kill Me. You tell lies. You are unkind to poor people. You pretend to love God, but while you are saying your prayers, you are thinking how good you are. Your hearts are full of wickedness. You are the children of the devil."[5]

Jesus wished them to turn from their wickedness. It grieved Him to see that they hated His Father, and that they would not turn from their wicked ways.[6]

The wicked people were angry with Jesus, and said, "God is not your Father."[7] But Jesus said, "He is My Father, and I came down from heaven, where He lives,[8] and I shall go back to Him some day."[9]

At last the people took up some stones to throw at Him, but Jesus did not choose to die yet, so He easily got away, and went to a place where they could not find Him.

There He stayed with His disciples a good while.[10]

Questions for Lesson 28

Did Jesus know that the wicked people would soon kill Him?
To whom did Jesus talk about His dying?
Were they sorry?
Why did many people hate Jesus?
Who is the father of liars?
How did the wicked people try to kill Jesus?
Did Jesus let them kill Him?
Why did He hide Himself in a place a great way off?

Scripture Verse

Where Jesus came from, and where he went.
'I came forth from the Father, and am come into the world: again, I leave the world, and go to the Father.' - (John 16:28).

Notes for Lesson 28

1. John 18:4.   2. John 10:18.
3. John 7:7.   4. John 5:42,44.
5. Luke 20:47; Matt. 15:8; Matt. 23:28; John 8:40,44.
6. See Mark 3:5; John 5:40.   7. John 5:18.
8. John 8:42,43.   9. John 6:62.
10. John 10:31,39,40.

* * * * * * * * * *

LESSON 29
LAZARUS
John 11:1 - 17

Jesus stayed with His disciples in a place by Himself. The wicked people who wanted to kill Him, could not find Him; but Jesus' friends knew where He was.

Jesus had more friends besides His disciples.

One of His friends was called Lazarus. Lazarus had two sisters; their names were Martha and Mary. These three all lived together. They all loved Jesus, and Jesus loved them. Jesus often uesd to come and see them, and sit in the house, and talk to them. Martha liked to make a fine dinner when Jesus came, but Mary liked to sit and listen to His sweet words.[1]

One day Lazarus became very ill.

Martha and Mary loved their brother Lazarus very much indeed. They knew that Jesus could make Lazarus well; so they sent a man to tell Jesus that Lazarus was sick.

The man went a great way to look for Jesus.

Lazarus grew worse and worse. At last he died. His friends wrapped white cloths round his face, and his arms and his legs, and put him in a great hole, and rolled a stone before it.

Martha and Mary waited and longed for Jesus to come.

Four days passed, and at last Jesus came.

Martha and Mary did not think that Jesus would make Lazarus alive again, for he had been dead so long; so they sat on the ground and cried.

When Martha heard that Jesus was on the road a little way off, she came to Jesus and said, "If you had been here, my brother would not have died; and even now you could make him alive."

Then Jesus said, "Your brother will rise again."

"Yes," said Martha, "I know he will rise again at the last day, when all the dead people rise."

Martha was afraid that Jesus would not choose to make Lazarus alive soon; but she knew that He was able to do it.

Martha went back to the house, and found Mary still sitting on the ground, and a great many friends round her.

Martha whispered in her ear, and told her that Jesus wanted to speak to her. So Martha and Mary went together, and found Jesus waiting for them on the road.

Mary's friends went with her, and they cried; and Mary cried very much indeed, and when she saw Jesus she fell down at His feet and said, "Lord, if you had been here my brother would not have died."

Jesus was very sorry to see her so unhappy, and to see so many people crying; He felt very sad indeed, and He was deeply moved.

Then Jesus said, "Where have you put Lazarus?"

Martha and Mary and their friends said, "Come and see;" and they showed Him the way.

As Jesus walked along, the tears rolled down His cheeks.

At last they came to the grave. It was a hole, and a very large stone was before the hole.

Then Jesus said, "Take away the stone."

Martha thought that Jesus was going to look at Lazarus lying dead; and she said, "Do not go in; his flesh has a bad smell by this time. He has been dead for four days." But Jesus told her to believe that He could make him alive.

Then they rolled away the stone.

Then Jesus lifted up His eyes to His Father in heaven, and thanked Him for helping Him to do wonderful things.

A great many people were standing by, looking at Jesus, and wondering what He would do.

Poor Martha and Mary were longing to see Lazarus alive again. Then Jesus spoke loudly saying, "Lazarus, come forth."

Lazarus heard, though he was dead; for the dead hear the voice of Jesus. He got up and walked to the door of the hole. His hands were tied with cloths, and a cloth was over his face.

But Jesus said, "Undo the cloths."

How pleased Martha and Mary must have been to see his face again! How they must have thanked the Lord Jesus for His kindness! The people who saw all this were surprised, and said, "Jesus must be the Son of God."

Questions for Lesson 29

Did Lazarus have any sisters?

What were their names?

Did Jesus ever come to their house and dine?

When Lazarus was sick, was Jesus with him, or far away?

Was Lazarus dead before Jesus came?

Did Martha think that Jesus could make Lazarus alive again?

Why did Jesus sigh and weep?

Where was dead Lazarus put?

What did Jesus say to Lazarus?

What clothes did Lazarus wear in the grave?

What did the people think of Jesus when they saw Him make Lazarus alive again?

Scripture Verse

God's care of the righteous.

'The righteous cry, and the Lord heareth, and delivereth them out of all their troubles.' - (Ps. 34:17).

Notes for Lesson 29

1. Luke 10:38 to end.

* * * * * * * * * *

LESSON 30
JESUS ENTERS JERUSALEM
Matt. 21:1 - 11, 14 - 17.

Which was the greatest miracle that Jesus ever did?

He made Lazarus alive again. Lazarus had been dead for four days. Many of the wicked people who hated Jesus heard of it; but they only hated Him the more. They said, "We must kill Him soon, or everyone will believe that He is the Son of God."

Jesus knew that they wanted to kill Him, and so He went again and hid Himself in a place that they did not know of. They looked for Him, but they could not find Him.

But could Jesus always stay in that little quiet place, where He was hidden with His disciples? No. He came down to die for us. He only waited till the time came for Him to die. Then He said to His disciples, "We must go to Jerusalem, and I will be laughed at, and beaten, and killed; but I will come out of My grave after three days."

The disciples did not like to hear this; but they chose to go with Jesus wherever He went.

Jesus walked quickly along the road; at last He came near Jerusalem. Then He stopped and said to His disciples, "I shall ride into Jerusalem upon a donkey." Jesus had no donkey of His own; He always walked from place to place. But Jesus could put it into a man's heart to lend Him one.

He said to two of His disciples, "Go along the road a little way, and you will see a donkey and her colt tethered, and a man standing near; bring the donkey and the colt to Me, for I know that the man will let them come."

So the two disciples went; when they had gone a little way they saw a donkey tied up, and a colt.

They began to untie them; but a man standing near said, "Why are you untying the donkey?"

They said, "The Lord needs them;" and then the man let them go. I suppose that man loved the Lord Jesus, and liked to lend Him his things.

The disciples brought the two donkeys to Jesus. They took off some of their clothes, and put them on the young donkey, and Jesus sat upon it.

A great many people came out of Jerusalem to see Jesus, for they had heard that He had made Lazarus alive again. The people began to praise Jesus, and call Him "King." They took off some of their clothes, and laid them down upon the road for the donkey to walk upon; and they picked branches off the trees that grew near, and laid them, too, on the road.

So Jesus came to the great town of Jerusalem; all the people came into the streets to look at Him, and even the little children began to praise Him, and to call Him "King." The proud men that hated Jesus were very angry at hearing all these praises. They did not like to hear Jesus praised. They came to Him and said, "Why do you let these children call you king?"

But Jesus liked to hear the children sing His praise, and he would not tell them to be silent. Jesus loved little children, and these little children loved Jesus.

Questions for Lesson 30

What did some of the people in Jerusalem wish to do to Jesus?

Did Jesus walk or ride into Jerusalem?

Where did the disciples find a donkey?

Why did so many of the people come to see Jesus when He was riding on the donkey?

What did the people lay upon the road?

How did the little children make the proud men angry?

Scripture Verse

The people who should praise God.

'Both young men, and maidens; old men and children: let them praise the name of the Lord...' - (Ps. 148:12,13).

* * * * * * * * * *

LESSON 31
THE TEMPLE

Luke 19:47,48; 20:19,20; 21:37,38.

There was a large place in Jerusalem, like a great church, called the Temple. It was white outside, and very beautiful. The doors were open all day, and people used to go in to pray to God. It was God's house; Jesus used often to be there with his disciples. Poor, blind, and lame people came to Him there, and Jesus cured them all, and talked to them about His Father.

The little children sang His praises in the Temple.

All day long Jesus taught the people about God, and they listened to what He said, and liked to hear Him.

The wicked and proud men came to the Temple to laugh at Jesus, and to speak rudely to Him; but He took it all without retaliating.

At night He left the Temple, and went out of the town to a high hill, where He prayed to God alone in the dark.

The wicked men longed to catch Jesus to kill Him. They said to each other, "How can we get Him? The people will not let us take hold of Him if they see us or we would go to the Temple to catch Him. If we could find Him alone in the dark, then we could tie him up, and take Him to the judge."

This is what the wicked people said to each other as they sat together.

Questions for Lesson 31

Where was the Temple?

What did people do in the Temple?

Did Jesus go there often?

Who used to come there to laugh at Jesus?

Where did Jesus go at night?

Why didn't the wicked men take Jesus when He was in the Temple?

Did the wicked men know where Jesus went at night?

Scripture Verse

Of wicked people's cruelty.

'The wicked watcheth the righteous, and seeketh to slay him.'
- (Ps. 37:32).

LESSON 32
JUDAS
John 12:6; Matt. 26:3,4, 14-16.

Jesus had twelve disciples.

Did they all love Him?

Peter loved Jesus, and John loved Him, and all the rest loved[1] Him except for one; his name was Judas. He did not love Jesus, but only pretended to love Him. He was like the devil.[2]

Did Jesus know how wicked Judas was? Yes; He saw into his heart; but the disciples thought Judas was good,[3] for Judas used to kiss the Lord Jesus, and speak kindly to Him, and talk about God like the rest.

But Judas loved something; he loved money. He wanted to get a great deal of money.

He was covetous, and he was a thief. The disciples had a bag, and when they had money, they put it in the bag; and all the disciples put their money in the same bag. But there was very little money in the bag, for they were very poor. Judas used to take care of the bag, and he used to steal some of the money, and keep it for himself; but no one found him out, or thought he was a thief, except Jesus, and he knew it well.

Judas was always thinking, "How shall I get money?"

One day, when the proud men were sitting together, Judas came in.

Judas said to them, "You want to find Jesus when He is alone; will you give me some money, if I show you where He goes at night?"

The proud people said, "Yes, we will."

Judas said, "How much money will you give me?"

They said, "Thirty pieces of silver."

Then Judas said, "Some night I will bring you to Jesus when He is alone."

The wicked people were very glad to hear this.

"Now," they thought, "we shall soon catch Him and kill Him."

Judas went back to Jesus, but he did not tell the disciples what he had done. Jesus knew what he had been doing, for Jesus could see all his thoughts, and He knew all that Judas did, both in the day and in the night. Yet Jesus did not tell Judas that He knew his wicked plans.

Questions for Lesson 32

Did *all* Jesus' disciples love Him?

Did Judas *say* that he did not love Jesus?

Did the other disciples know that Judas did not love Jesus?

Did Jesus know it?

Was Judas a thief?

What did Judas love more than anything else?

What did Judas promise the wicked people he would do if they would give him money?

How much money did they promise to give him?

Did Jesus know that Judas meant to show the wicked people where He was at night?

Scripture Verse

God can see all things.

'..the darkness hideth not from thee: but the night shineth as the day...' - (Ps. 139:12).

Notes for Lesson 32

[1] John 16:27.   [2] John 6:70.

[3.] This is evident, from the disciples trusting Judas with the bag, and from their failing to suspect him of treachery to their Lord, when one of their number was accused.

SECTION 6

THE LAST MEAL

Introduction

In this section we will learn about what is often called The Lord's Supper when Jesus got together with his twelve disciples to celebrate the Jewish Passover feast. The Passover was a special celebration when the Jewish people gathered as families and used a meal to remember how God had brought their ancestors out of slavery in Egypt. Jesus used the bread and wine at the meal to help people think about what he was about to do on the cross.

However, it was also a time when Judas Iscariot, one of the disciples, had planned to betray Jesus and another, Peter, would shortly afterwards say he never knew him.

Some Suggestions for Study

Think of special meals that people have today, birthday parties, Christmas dinners, or other celebrations. At the beginning of each lesson think of a particular meal that you remember well. Ask yourself why you remember it. Finish by thanking God for such times and particularly for what the Last Supper means to us.

LESSON 33
THE LAST SUPPER - PART 1.
Luke 22:7 -14; John 13:1-17.

Jesus said to His disciples, "I am going to be killed soon, but before I die I shall eat a supper with you in Jerusalem."

Then Jesus said to Peter and John, "Go and get the supper ready;" but they said "Where shall we get it ready?" for Jesus had no house in Jerusalem; but Jesus knew how to find a room.

So Jesus said to Peter and John, "Go into Jerusalem, and you will meet a man carrying a jug; go after him; he will go into a house. The master of the house will lend Me a room. Tell him that I am going to die, and that I want to eat a supper with My disciples."

Then Peter and John went into Jerusalem.

Whom did they meet? - A man carrying a jug.

They followed him. He went into a house. Peter and John went in after him, and they said to the master of the house, "Jesus wants a room to eat supper in with His disciples, before He dies."

Then the master took them upstairs, and showed them a large room, with a table in it, and seats all round the table, and a jug, and a basin to wash their feet in, and a cup and dishes.

Then Peter and John got some bread and wine and other things, and made the supper ready; and they went back and told Jesus (who was a little way in the country) that supper was ready. So Jesus and all His disciples came to the house in the evening; they went upstairs, and they all sat down.

Jesus loved John more than all the rest, and John sat next to Jesus.

After they had been a little while at supper, Jesus got up

and took a towel and tied it round His waist, and He took a jug and poured water into a basin, and He began to wash His disciples' feet, and to wipe them with the towel round His waist.

But when He came to Peter, Peter said, "You shall never wash my feet."

Peter thought it was too kind of Jesus to wash his feet, as if He were a servant; but Jesus was not proud, but loved to be kind to His disciples.

Then Jesus said to Peter, "If I do not wash you, you cannot be Mine; but I have made you clean already." Jesus had made Peter's heart clean.

Then Peter was glad that Jesus washed his feet.

All the disciples had clean hearts, except Judas, and his heart was full of wickedness: Satan was in it. Yet Jesus washed Judas' feet. He was kind even to wicked Judas, who hated Him.

When Jesus had washed all the disciples' feet, He sat down again, and began to talk to them.

He said, "Do you know what I have done to you? I have washed your feet, though I am your Lord and Master. I wish to teach you to be as kind to each other as I have been to you."

Questions for Lesson 33

Did Jesus have a house in Jerusalem?

How did He get a room to eat supper in with His disciples before He died?

Whom did He send to find the room?

How did Peter and John find out which house they were to go to?

What things were in the room?

Who sat next to Jesus at supper?

How many people were at the supper?
Why did Jesus pour water into a basin?
Why didn't Peter like Jesus to wash his feet?
Had Jesus made His disciples' hearts clean?
Was Judas' heart clean?
Why did Jesus wash His disciples feet?
What commandment did Jesus give to His disciples?

Scripture Verse

Christ's last command.

'This is my commandment, that ye love one another, as I have loved you.' - (John 15:12).

* * * * * * * * * *

LESSON 34
THE LAST SUPPER - PART 2.
John 13:21 - 30.

You know the wicked thing that Judas meant to do. Jesus knew that he would bring the wicked people to take Him and kill Him. Jesus had been very kind to Judas, and Jesus was sorry that he was so wicked.

As Jesus was sitting at supper, and all the twelve disciples sitting round, He said, "One of you will give Me to the wicked men to be killed! One of you, My disciples."

The disciples were very sorry, and Peter said, "Is it I?" and John said, "Is it I?" and each of them said, "Is it I?" but Jesus did not tell them which.

Now John was leaning his head on Jesus' chest, and Peter whispered to John and said, "Ask the Lord who will show the wicked people where He is?"

So John whispered and said, "Who is it?"

And Jesus said, "The one that dips the bread in the dish with Me."

For there was a dish of sauce on the table, and Jesus dipped His bread in it, and as He dipped it, one of the disciples put his hand in the dish too. Who was it?

Judas; he dipped his bread in the dish with Jesus. So John knew who it was that was so wicked.

Then Jesus said to Judas, "Go and do what you mean to do."

And Judas got up and went out of the room.

Where did he go?

He went to the wicked people, to bring them to Jesus in the dark.

But the disciples thought he was going to buy something, or give money to the poor.

Questions for Lesson 34

What did Jesus say, at supper, that one of His disciples would do?

Who asked Jesus to tell him who it was?

Who dipped his hand in the dish with Jesus?

Why did Judas go out of the room?

What did the disciples think He was going to do?

Scripture Verse

God alone knows us best.

'...for thou, even thou only, knowest the hearts of all the children of men.' - (1 Kings 8:39).

LESSON 35
THE LAST SUPPER - PART 3.
Matt. 26:26-36. John 14:1 - 4; 18:1 - 3

After supper Jesus took some bread and broke it in little bits, and gave a piece to each of the disciples, and said, "This is My body: I am going to die; eat this, and think of Me."

Then Jesus poured some wine into a cup, and told them all to drink out of it. He said, "This is My blood; I shall soon bleed and die: drink this, and think of Me."

Jesus said, "I shall not eat supper with you again before I die. I am going to My Father; I must leave you, but I shall come back again."

Then they all sang a hymn.

Afterwards Jesus got up from the table and went downstairs into the street, and the disciples followed Him. It was dark; but Jesus talked to them as they went along. He said, "I am going to die to-night, and you will all leave Me."

But Peter said, "I will not leave you; I will go to prison with you; I will die with you; but I will never leave you."

Jesus said to him, "Yes, you will, Peter; you will say that you do not know Me; you will say that you are not My friend. This night, Peter, you will say so, before the cock crows." (For cocks crow in the morning when it is light.)

Jesus talked sweetly to His disciples. He said, "Do not be sorry because I am going away. I shall go back to My Father, and I shall soon come back to you. When I am in heaven, I shall get ready a place in heaven for you. I command you to love one another, and I will send the Holy Spirit to comfort you."

At last Jesus came to a garden. He had often been to that garden with His disciples, and wicked Judas knew the place.

Where was Judas now?

He was with the wicked proud men.

You will soon hear how he came to the garden, and how he brought the servants of the wicked men with him. For those wicked men meant to send their servants to catch Jesus.

Questions for Lesson 35

What did Jesus break into pieces and give to His disciples?

What did He give them to drink?

What was the bread like?

What was the wine like?

Where did Jesus go after supper?

What did He tell His disciples as He walked along the road?

What did Peter say he would do, if Jesus was killed or taken prisoner?

What did Jesus tell Peter that he would say?

Where would Jesus go after He was killed?

Would Jesus forget His disciples when He was in heaven?

What did Jesus say he would send into their hearts?

Where did Jesus take His disciples?

Scripture Verse

What Jesus said he would do for his disciples in heaven.
'...I go to prepare a place for you.' - (John 14:2).

SECTION 7

THE FINAL NIGHT

Introduction
This section is about the final night before Jesus' crucifixion. In many ways, it is a reflection on where people's loyalties lie - Jesus' loyalty to His Father's will, Peter's struggle to be loyal to Jesus, Pontius Pilate's effort to be loyal to Roman justice, and Judas' personal dilemma following his disloyalty to Jesus.

Some Suggestions for Study
Think of people who demand your loyalty eg. members of a club or Sunday school, or a group of friends. After each lesson, think about the person in the story and their attitude towards following God. Think about what you would have done and whether your loyalty to Jesus always comes first.

LESSON 36
THE GARDEN
Matt. 26:30 - 57;   John 18:1 - 12.

When Jesus harrived at the garden, He told all His disciples to stop in one place till He came back, except three whom He took with Him.

Who were they? Peter, James, and John. He took them further into the garden and then said to them, "I feel very sad indeed. I am going to pray. Stay here. Do not go to sleep, but pray while I am praying."

Then Jesus went a little way off by Himself, and fell upon the ground, and began to pray to His Father to help Him. He ended His prayer by saying, "O Father, let Your will be done, not mine."[1]

He was full of sorrow and troubled and prayed very earnestly. Then He got up and went back to Peter, and James, and John, but He found them asleep. He woke them, and told them to pray.

Jesus went back and asked His Father to help Him in His great sorrow; then He came back to His disciples, but they had fallen asleep again.

Then Jesus prayed again, and His Father sent an angel from heaven to comfort Him. I do not know what the angel said, but I know he loved Him, and could speak encouraging words to Him, and tell Him how His Father loved Him. The angel did not stay long; he soon went back to God.

Then Jesus came again to His disciples, and found them still asleep. He woke them, and told them to get up; "For my betrayer," He said, "is near."

While Jesus was saying this, a great many people were seen

walking in the garden. They were the servants of the proud men in Jerusalem. They had swords, and sticks, and lanterns in their hands. Judas went before them to show them where Jesus was. He came up slyly to Jesus, and gave Him a kiss.

Jesus knew what Judas was doing, and He said, "Friend, why do you come here? And why do you kiss Me?"

Jesus did not run away, but He went up to the wicked men, and said, "Who are you looking for?"

They said, "For Jesus." He said, "I am He."

When He said that, all the wicked people moved back and fell to the ground. Jesus could have run away; but He chose to stay, so that He might die for sinners.

The wicked people soon got up; God let them get up; but Jesus said to them, "If you want to have Me you must let My disciples go away."

It was kind of Jesus to think of them, and they were frightened and glad to get away; they did not wish to die with Jesus.

Peter, wanting to resist, took a sword and cut off one of the wicked men's ears. However, Jesus said, "Put your sword away. If I were to pray now to My Father, He would send thousands of angels to help Me."[1] Then Jesus touched the man's ear, and made it well.

Why didn't Jesus pray to God to send the angels?

Because He chose to die to save us. If the angels had come, and taken Jesus back to heaven, we would all have gone to hell.

Peter and all the rest of the disciples ran away, and left Jesus quite alone with the wicked men. They took ropes, and tied His hands and feet, and they led Him away into Jerusalem, and He went along meekly as a lamb.

Questions for Lesson 36

When Jesus was in the garden, did He take *all* His disciples
with Him to another part of the garden?

How many did He take with Him?

What did Jesus tell them to do while He was praying?

What did Jesus pray to His Father about?

Was He very unhappy?

Did Peter, James and John pray while Jesus was praying?

How many times did Jesus come back to Peter, James and
John?

Who came from heaven to comfort Him?

Who came into the garden at last?

Why did Judas kiss Jesus?

Did Jesus know why Judas kissed Him?

What kind of name did Jesus call Judas?

Did Jesus run away from the wicked men?

Who made the wicked people fall down upon the ground?

Did they get up again soon?

Did the disciples run away?

What did Peter cut off with his sword?

Did Jesus wish Peter to fight for Him?

What was it Jesus did to the man's ear?

Where did the wicked people take Jesus?

What was Jesus like, when He went so meekly with them?

Scripture Verse

How meek Jesus was when he died for us.

'...he is brought as a lamb to the slaughter, and as a sheep
before her shearers is dumb, so he openeth not his mouth.' -
(Isa. 53:7).

Notes for Lesson 36

[1.] John 18:11.

LESSON 37
PETER'S DENIAL.
Matt. 26:57 to end.

The wicked, proud men who hated Jesus had sat up all night. They had sent their servants with some soldiers to fetch Jesus. They were probably in a fine house, seated on seats round the room, talking together, and impatient for Jesus to be brought.

They said one to another, "We will have Him killed when He comes - we will take Him to the judge."

At last Jesus came in with the wicked servants. The proud men were glad to see Him. They made Him stand up in the midst of the large room. Then they spoke roughly. "Are you the Son of God?" they asked.

"Yes," said Jesus. "I am; and one day you will see Me coming in the clouds with the angels."

Then the wicked men were angry.

"Do you hear what He says?" they cried out. "He calls Himself the Son of God; He must be taken to the judge to be killed."

Jesus stood meekly all this while, and hardly spoke a word.

What had happened to the disciples? They had run away.

Did Peter run away? He said he would die with Jesus, but he ran away too. At last Peter thought, "I will go and look for Jesus; I should like to see what the wicked men are doing to Him."

So Peter came to Jerusalem, and into the fine house. He came into the middle of the courtyard; the servants were sitting round a fire. He hoped that nobody would know that he was one of Jesus' disciples, in case he was killed. But as he was sitting by the fire, warming himself, a maid said to him, "You are one of Jesus' disciples."

Then Peter was frightened, and said, "No, I am not; I do not know the man you speak of."

He got up, and went outside the gateway, but another maid said to him, "I am sure you are one of the disciples of Jesus."

"No", said Peter, "I am not."

Later some of the bystanders again challenged him saying, "We are certain that you are one of the disciples, because you are a Galilean." Another said, "I saw you in the garden."

Then Peter began to swear, and to say that he was not. While he was speaking so wickedly he heard a cock crow.

Then he saw Jesus look straight at him and he remembered what Jesus had said. It must have been such a look!

Peter felt very sorry; he felt as if his heart would break, and he went out of the house, and began to cry very much indeed. For he really did love Jesus; only Satan had tempted him to be so wicked as to say he did not know Him.

However, Christ had prayed for Peter, that Satan might not get his soul.[1]

Questions for Lesson 37

Had the proud men gone to the garden *themselves,* or had they sent their servants?

What had they been doing all night?

When Jesus came to Jerusalem where did He stand?

Did they ask Him if He was the Son of God?

Did He say that He was?

What did the wicked proud men say must be done to Jesus?

Where was Peter all this time?

Could Peter see Jesus?

Did Peter wish people to know that he was one of Jesus'
disciples?

Why not?

Did any one ask Peter who he was?

What did Peter say?

How many times did people ask Peter who he was?

What did Peter hear that made him feel how naughty he had
been?

What was it Peter did, after Jesus looked at him?

Did Peter really love Jesus?

Who had often prayed for Peter?

Did Satan have his soul?

Scripture Verse

How Peter repented of his sin.

'And the Lord turned, and looked upon Peter..... And Peter
went out, and wept bitterly.' - (Luke 22:61,62).

Notes for Lesson 37

[1.] Luke 22:31,32.

* * * * * * * * * *

LESSON 38
PONTIUS PILATE

John 18:22 to end; Matt. 26:67, 68; John 19:1 - 16.

All night long, Jesus stood in the great room; He heard all
Peter said, and that must have grieved Him. The wicked people
were like lions and tigers, and Jesus like a lamb. They looked
at Him as if they hated Him.[1]

Once when He spoke, a servant slapped His face, but He
bore this meekly.

The judge was not up yet, for it was night; so the wicked people were forced to wait till the morning.

That night the servants came round Jesus and beat Him, and pushed Him, and laughed at Him, and even spat in His face.

When the morning came, the wicked people said, "Now we will bring Him to the judge."

So they went out of their fine house and took Jesus with them. The judge sat upon a high seat in the street. His name was Pontius Pilate. The judge did not know Jesus. The judge said, "What has He done?"

The wicked people said, "He calls Himself a king."

Then Pilate said to Jesus, "Are you a king?" and Jesus said, "Yes, I am." But Pilate thought that He looked very good, and he did not like to punish Him.

Then the wicked men made a great noise, and said, "You must crucify Him!"

"No," said Pilate, "I will beat Him, and that will be enough." So Pilate gave Jesus to some soldiers, who took Him into a house and beat Him with knotted ropes (this way of beating is called scourging), and all the blood ran down His back. Then the cruel soldiers laughed at Him, because He said He was a king. They took off His own clothes, and put some fine clothes on Him, such as kings wear, purple and red.

Then they said, "We must put a crown on His head." So they took prickly thorns, sharp like pins, and twisted them together, and made a crown, and put it on His head.

They said, "He must have a sceptre" (for kings hold something called a sceptre in their hands), so they put a reed in His hand for a sceptre; then they took it from Him, and beat Him on the head: and they knelt down to Him laughing, and said, "O king! O king!"

Pilate saw the soldiers tormenting Him, and he brought Jesus into the street, where the wicked people were, and he showed Jesus to them, and said, "Look at your King!"

Pilate hoped they would be satisfied to see Him so ill-treated; blood upon His forehead from the thorns, and His back whipped, and dressed in fine clothes to make fun of Him; but the wicked people were cruel.

"No," said they: "Crucify Him! Crucify Him!" All the people cried out, "Crucify Him!" though Jesus had always been so kind to them.

"Will you crucify your king?" said Pilate.

"He shall not be our king!" the people said. There was a very great noise in the street, from the people all speaking at once.

Then Pilate thought he would please the wicked people, and he said, "Take Him and crucify Him." Then the people were glad. But first the soldiers took the fine clothes off Jesus, and put His own clothes on Him again.

How wicked it was of Pilate to let Him be crucified! Pilate thought Jesus was good, yet he let Him be killed to please the people.

Questions for Lesson 38

Did Jesus stand a long time before the wicked people?

How did one of the servants behave to Him?

When did the wicked men take Him to the judge?

What did the servants put over His face?

Where was the judge sitting?

What was the judge's name?

Did the judge wish to hurt Jesus?

What did the wicked people say that Jesus had called Himself?

Was He a king?

What is scourging?
Why did the soldiers laugh at Him?
What clothes did they put on Him?
What did they put on His head?
What did they put in His hand?
What is a sceptre?
Why did Pilate tell the wicked people to look at Jesus?
Did the people make a great noise?
What did Pilate at last say should be done to Jesus?
Why did Pilate allow Jesus to be crucified?

Scripture Verse

How Jesus was treated before he died.
'...I hid not my face from shame and spitting.' - (Isa. 50:6).

Notes for Lesson 38

1. Ps.22:13; Ps. 35:16.

* * * * * * * * * *

LESSON 39
DEATH OF JUDAS
Matt. 27:3 - 5.

Where was Judas all this while? The wicked people had given him the money - thirty pieces of silver; but Judas could not be happy.

"Ah!" thought he, "I have killed my good Master! What a wicked thing I have done!"

Judas felt that he could not like the money; he could not bear to keep it, because he had done such a wicked thing to get it. So Judas went to look for the wicked men. They had been sitting up all night talking against Jesus; but now they were in God's house - the Temple.

Judas brought the thirty pieces of silver in his hands, and threw them down on the floor near the wicked men. Judas said, "I have done a very wicked thing."

But the men did not care for *that;* all they wanted was to get Jesus killed.

They picked up the pieces of silver from the floor, and went and bought a field with the money.

And where did Judas go?

He went out to the field to kill himself. He did not go and ask Jesus to forgive him, but went out and hung himself. I suppose he tied a rope round his neck, and fastened the rope to a tree. Afterwards he fell down from the tree, and his body burst, and his blood was poured on the ground.[1] O, what a horrible sight it must have been! But it was more horrible to think where Judas' soul might have gone.

It was very wicked of Judas to hang himself.

Judas is in his place;[2] Jesus will judge him on the last day.

Questions for Lesson 39

Was Judas happy when he got the thirty pieces of silver?
What did he do with them?
How did Judas kill himself?
Where is Judas now?

Scripture Verse

The misery of the wicked.
'There is no peace, saith my God, to the wicked.' - (Isa. 57:21).

Notes for Lesson 39

[1.] Acts 1:18.   [2.] Acts 1:25.

SECTION 8

JESUS DIES

Introduction
In this section we will focus upon Jesus' death on the cross and his burial.

Some Suggestions for Study
Find a piece of music that you might say is sad. Play it at some point before, during or after each of the lessons in this section. Thank God that 'although Friday is here Sunday is coming!'

LESSON 40
THE CROSS - PART 1
Luke 23:26 - 34.

The wicked people were very glad when Pilate said Jesus was to be crucified. They made a cross of two big pieces of wood like boards, and made Jesus carry it. They took Him out of Jerusalem into the country. The wicked people came with Him.

Jesus was so weak that He could hardly walk, and the cross was so heavy that He could not carry it. He would have dropped down on the way, if a man had not helped Him to carry the cross.

There were a few people who were sorry for the Lord Jesus.

Some women, who loved Him very much, came crying after Him. Jesus heard them crying, and He turned round and spoke very kindly to them.

He said, "Do not cry for me; cry for yourselves, and for your children." Why did Jesus tell them to cry for themselves? Ah! Jesus knew how God would one day punish the people in Jerusalem for their wickedness.

At last Jesus came to the top of a hill. Then the soldiers made Jesus lie upon His cross, and they put nails in His hands, and nails in His feet. So they nailed Him to the cross. Then the soldiers made a hole in the ground, and stuck the cross in it.

They had taken off Jesus' clothes; and when He was on the cross, four soldiers tore the clothes in four pieces, and each took a piece; but when they looked at His coat they said, "We will not tear it, because there is no seam in it"; then one of the soldiers took it for himself. So the wicked people took everything away from Jesus.

Was Jesus very angry with them? No; He was as meek as a lamb. He prayed to His Father while He was upon the cross; He could not lift up His hands, but He could speak to God. He prayed for these wicked people, and said, "Father, forgive them; for they do not know what they are doing."

Questions for Lesson 40

Who carried Jesus' cross?

Could Jesus carry it by Himself?

Who came after Jesus, crying, because he was going to die?

What did Jesus say to these kind women?

What did the wicked men do to Jesus when He came to the top of the hill?

Who took Jesus' clothes?

Did they tear them all?

Whom did Jesus ask His Father to forgive?

Should we forgive people who are unkind to us?

Scripture Verse

Jesus' prayer for those who crucified him.

'...Father, forgive them, for they know not what they do...' - (Luke 23:34).

* * * * * * * * * *

LESSON 41
THE CROSS - PART 2
Luke 23:35 - 43.

Pontius Pilate wrote these words on the top of Jesus' cross; "This is the King of the Jews."

Who were the Jews? The people who lived in Jerusalem were called Jews.

All the wicked people laughed when they read these words; they shook their heads, and pouted their lips at Jesus, and said, "If you are the Son of God come down from the cross."

Could Jesus have come down? He could do everything; but He chose to stay to die for sinners.

The wicked people said, "If God loved Him, He would not leave Him to die on the cross."

But His Father let Him die to save us.

There was a cross on each side of Jesus, and a thief nailed upon each cross. One of these thieves laughed at Jesus; He said, "Why do you not save us, if you are the Son of God?"

The other thief was sorry for his sins, and he believed in Jesus. The thief who was sorry said to the other thief, "We have been naughty, we deserve to be crucified; but this man is good." Then He spoke to Jesus, and said, "Remember me when you come to be king."

And Jesus said, "You shall be with Me in heaven to-day." So Christ heard the poor thief's prayer, and He died to save all who believe that He is the Son of God.

If you go to heaven, you will see that poor thief.

Questions for Lesson 41

What did Pontius Pilate write upon the cross?
Did the wicked people come to see Jesus upon the cross?
What did they say to Jesus?
Why did Jesus not come down from the cross?
How many people were crucified with Jesus?
Did both thieves go to heaven?
What did one of the thieves ask Jesus to do?
Did he ask Jesus to save him from dying on the cross?

Scripture Verse

What we must do if we wish God to forgive us.
'If we confess our sins, God is faithful and just to forgive us our sins...' - (1 John 1:9).

* * * * * * * * * *

LESSON 42
THE CROSS - PART 3
John 19:25 - 30; Matt. 27:45 - 54.

Jesus' mother, Mary, stood near the cross. She came to see her Son die. She was very sorry; she felt her heart full of pain at the sight.[1]

She loved her dear, good Son, who had been kind to her ever since He was a baby, and had never done one thing wrong, and she knew He was the Son of God. Jesus was sorry to see His mother's grief.

John had come to the cross, and he was standing near Mary.

Jesus wished John to take care of His mother, now that He was going to leave her. So He said to His mother, "Behold your son!" Then He said to John, "Behold your mother!" John knew what Jesus meant, and he took Mary to be his mother, and made her live with him. Jesus loved His mother, and thought of her when He was dying.

Jesus was full of pain, and it was very hot. He said, "I thirst!" and the soldiers took a sponge, and dipped it in vinegar, and put it on a reed, and gave it to Jesus.

Jesus tasted the vinegar, and said, "It is finished!" and then He died. His spirit went to His Father, but His body hung upon the cross.

It was three o'clock in the afternoon when Jesus died. He had been nailed to the cross all day. Before Jesus died God made it very dark, to show He was angry with the wicked people. And God made the earth shake, and the people were frightened; and when Jesus was dead, some of them said, "This must have been the Son of God."

Questions for Lesson 42

Where was Jesus' mother, Mary, when He was on the cross?
Who stood near Mary?
Who took care of her after Jesus was crucified?
What did the soldiers give Jesus to drink?
What did Jesus say just before He died?
What time was it when Jesus died?
What frightened the people just before He died?

Scripture Verse

How Christ was treated when thirsty upon the cross.
'..and in my thirst they gave me vinegar to drink.' - (Ps. 69:21).

Notes for Lesson 42

[1.] Luke 2:35.

LESSON 43
THE SOLDIERS
John 19:32 - 37.

At last the soldiers came to see if Jesus and the two thieves were dead, that they might bury them before night. The soldiers looked at one thief, and they saw that he was not dead; so they broke his legs, and that killed him. Then they looked at the other thief, and they saw that he was not dead; so they broke his legs. Then they looked at Jesus, and they saw that He was dead, so they did not break His legs; but one of the soldiers took a long stick with a sharp point at the end, called a spear, and put it in His side; and out of His side blood and water came flowing upon the ground. John was standing near, and He saw the blood poured out.

Do you remember how Jesus, at supper the night before, had poured wine into a cup, and said, "This is My blood, which is shed for sinners?" Now His blood was poured out.

The spear made a hole in Jesus' side. There was a hole in His side, and a hole in each hand, and a hole in each foot; and His forehead was pricked with thorns, and His eyes had shed many tears, and blood had come from His skin. All this He suffered for us, that God might forgive us our sins.[1]

Questions for Lesson 43

How did the soldiers kill the thieves?
Why did they kill them so soon?
Why didn't the soldiers break the legs of Jesus?
What did they put into the side of Jesus?
What is a spear?
What came out of His side?
What had Jesus poured out once at supper, and said, "This is My blood."
Why did Jesus shed His blood on the cross?

Scripture Verse

What takes away sin.
'...and the blood of Jesus Christ, his Son, cleanseth us from all sin.' - (1 John 1:7).

Notes for Lesson 43

[1.] Eph. 1:7.

LESSON 44
THE GRAVE.

John 19:38 to the end; Luke 23:55,56; Matt. 27:60.

There was one rich man who loved Jesus; his name was Joseph (not Mary's husband, this was another Joseph); he had a garden, and in the garden he had made a grave; perhaps he meant to be buried there himself when he came to die.

But now Joseph thought, "I should like to put the Lord Jesus in my grave." It was a very nice grave, and no one had ever been put there yet.

So Joseph went to Pontius Pilate and said, "I want the dead body of Jesus; may I take it down from the cross, and keep it myself?"

And Pilate said, "Yes; you may have it."

Then Joseph was glad. He brought some nice, white, clean linen. What do you think that was for? To wrap Jesus in. And he brought some spices (sweet-smelling things, that grow out of the ground), and he brought some men with him, and they took the nails out of Jesus' hands and feet, and took His body down from the cross. Then Joseph wrapped a cloth round His head, and another cloth round His waist, and he put sweet spices on Him; and then some men carried Him along to Joseph's garden.

In the garden there was a high place called a rock, and a hole in the rock, like a hole in the wall; and they walked into this large dark hole, and they laid Jesus down quite alone. Now He was at rest; He felt no pain, no sorrow; the wicked people were not near; and there lay the Lord in His quiet grave. The men took a very large stone and stopped up the hole, so that nobody could come in. No beast, no bird, could touch the

Lord Jesus. There were trees and flowers near Him in this sweet garden, and there were angels there watching over Him, though no one could see them.

Where were the poor women who loved Jesus?

They had been looking at Him on the cross. How they must have cried when they saw Him bleed, and heard Him cry out to God!

The poor women had seen the men take Him down from the cross. They had followed the men into the garden; they had seen Him put so carefully in His grave.

Then they went home to prepare spices and ointments for Jesus' body.

Questions for Lesson 44

Who put Jesus into his own grave?

Where was the grave?

Whom did Joseph ask to let him have Jesus' body?

What did Joseph wrap it in?

What did he put round Jesus' head and waist?

What was put before the grave?

Did any one see where Jesus was laid?

What did the women make when they went home?

Scripture Verse

What became of Jesus' body after he was crucified.
'And when Joseph had taken the body he wrapped it in a clean linen cloth, and laid it in his own new tomb...' -
(Matt. 27:59,60).

SECTION 9

JESUS IS ALIVE

Introduction

This section concentrates on the wonderful fact that Jesus rose from the dead. We will see how, after spending time reassuring his followers, Jesus ascended to heaven, where he waits to return for those who love him.

Some Suggestions for Study

Find a piece of music that you might say is happy. Play it at some point before, during or after each of the lessons in this section. Think about what Jesus did. Thank God for His love in sending His son to save us.

LESSON 45
THE RESURRECTION.
Mark 16:1 - 6; Luke 24:3 - 10; Matt. 28:9,10.

One morning very early, when Jesus had been dead only two days, the poor women came into the garden. It was not quite light yet; for the sun was just rising.

As the women walked along with their ointment they said to each other, "How shall we get into the grave? The men put a large stone before it; the stone is so big, we cannot roll it away." The women did not know what to do.

At last they came to the grave, but the stone was rolled away. The women were surprised. Then they were afraid some wicked people had rolled it away, and stolen the body of Jesus.

This made them very sad; they looked into the grave, and saw that Jesus was not there. Soon they saw two beautiful angels standing by them. Their faces were bright like the sun, their clothes whiter than snow.

The women trembled when they saw the angels; but the angels spoke sweetly and kindly to them, saying, "Do not be afraid; we know that you are looking for Jesus. He is not here now; He is alive. Do you not remember how He said He would come to life again, after He had been crucified? Come. Look at the place where Jesus lay. Run and tell His disciples that he is alive. They shall see Him very soon."

The women were very glad; they ran to tell the disciples. But as they ran, whom do you think they saw? Jesus Himself! He did not look as He once had looked; no tears were on His cheeks; they were all wiped away.[1] He was not weak and faint as when He carried His cross; He could not be sick any more; nor could He ever die again.[2]

The women were so pleased to see Him! They knelt down on the ground, and held His feet, that He might not go away, and they called Him their Lord and their God. Yet still they felt a little afraid; but Jesus told them not to be afraid. Jesus said, "Go tell My brothers that I shall soon see them again."

Whom did Jesus call His brothers? His disciples. He had forgiven them for having run away when the wicked men took Him. The poor women ran, as Jesus had told them, to the disciples, and said, "We have seen angels! We have seen the Lord Jesus! He is walking about, and you will see Him soon." But the disciples would not believe the women.

Questions for Lesson 45

When did the women come to the grave?
Why did they come?
Who rolled away the large stone?
How did the angels look?
Were the women pleased when they saw them?
What did the angels tell the women?
To whom did the women run to tell what they had seen?
Whom did the women see as they went along?
What did the women do when they saw Jesus?
Had Jesus forgiven His disciples for having left Him alone?
Did the disciples believe that the women had seen Jesus?

Scripture Verse

Christ's own words after he rose from the dead.
'I am he that liveth, and was dead; and, behold, I am alive for evermore...' - (Rev. 1:18).

Notes for Lesson 45
[1.] Ps. 21:6.   [2.] Rom. 6:9.

LESSON 46
MARY MAGDALENE.
John 20:1 - 19.

I have told you of two Marys; Mary, the mother of Jesus, and another Mary, the sister of Lazarus. But there was another still, called Mary Magdalene. She came very early to the grave, before the other women came. She looked in the grave, but saw no angels; so she came running back, and told Peter and John that Jesus was not in His grave. "I am afraid," said Mary Magdalene, "that some wicked people have taken Him away, and that we shall not be able to find Him."

So Peter and John began to run as fast as they could, but John ran the fastest, and he came first to the grave. He stooped down, and peeped in, and he saw the clothes lying in the grave.

Soon after Peter came, and he went down into the grave, and he saw the clothes neatly folded, and the cloth that was round Jesus' head lying in a place by itself. Then John went in too; and John thought of what Jesus had said about being alive again.

"It is all true," thought John; "He is alive, and has left His grave."

Then Peter and John came out of the grave, and went to their own house; but they saw no angels, nor did they see Jesus.

Where was Mary Magdalene all this time? She was standing crying outside the grave; she was quite alone, for Peter and John had gone home.

At last she stooped down and looked into the grave, and she saw a beautiful sight; two angels, one sitting where Jesus' head had been, and one where His feet had been!

The angels said to Mary, "Why do you cry?" but still she

went on crying, and said, "Some people have taken away the Lord Jesus, and I cannot find Him."

When she had said this, she heard a man behind her saying, "Why do you cry?"

She did not know who it was that spoke; she thought, it was the gardener. "If you have taken Him," she said, "tell me where you have put Him, and I will take Him away."

The man said, "Mary!" She knew that voice, and turning round she looked, and saw that it was Jesus. How glad she was to see her Lord and Master, whom she loved! But Jesus could not stay with her. He told her to go and tell His dear disciples that He was alive. "I am soon going up to My Father in heaven; but I shall see My disciples first."

Mary Magdalene came and told the disciples. They were all crying; but they would not believe what Mary said.

Mary was glad that she had gone to look for Jesus. She was the first of all the people who saw Jesus after He was alive again.[1]

Questions for Lesson 46

How many Marys have I told you of?
Who came very early to the grave of Jesus?
Which two disciples ran to the grave of Jesus?
Who got there first?
Which of them went into the grave first?
What did Peter and John see in the grave?
Did John believe that Jesus was alive again?
Did Peter and John see Jesus, or angels?
Who stood alone, crying, by the grave?
What did she see when she looked in?
Why did Mary Magdalene cry?
Who was the man who spoke to her kindly?

Was he the gardener?

Did Jesus stay with Mary?

Who was the first person that saw Jesus after He was alive again?

Scripture Verse

The happiness of the righteous.

'Be glad in the Lord, and rejoice, ye righteous...' - (Ps. 32:11).

Notes for Lesson 46

[1.] Mark 16:9.

* * * * * * * * * *

LESSON 47.
THE TWO FRIENDS

Luke 24:13 - 48.

It was early in the morning that the women went to look for Jesus. In the evening two good men were taking a walk together in the country. As they walked, they talked about Jesus. They had not seen Him since He was alive again; they did not know He was alive. They talked about His dying on the cross. It made them very sad to speak about it.

At last a man came and spoke to them; they thought he was a stranger; yet he seemed to be a kind man.

He said, "Why do you cry? I see you are talking of something very sad."

"Yes," said these good men, "we are talking of something sad. Did you never hear of Jesus; what wonderful things He did; how He cured the blind, and dumb, and sick; and how he taught people about God, and all the people loved Him; but at last He was crucified? We thought He had been the Son of

God, but now we are afraid He was not, for He is dead, and we are afraid that we shall never see Him again."

The kind stranger was sorry to see these good men cry. He began to talk to them, and to tell them that Jesus was the Son of God, and that He had been crucified to save men, and that He would rise again, and go back to His Father.

This kind stranger said a great deal more. He knew all the verses in the Bible, and told these men a great many things they did not know. They liked to listen to the stranger; they did not feel so sad while he was talking.

At last these men came to their own house: it was in the country. The stranger seemed as if he was going on; but the two good men said to him, "Please, stay at our house; it is getting dark. Come and eat with us, and sleep here; please, come in."

Then the stranger said he would come in.

The men went into a room, where there was a supper. They all three sat down together round the table. The stranger took some bread and broke it, and began to pray to God; and then the two men found out who the stranger was.

"It is the Lord!" they cried; and so it was. They looked towards Him, but they could see Him no more. He had not opened the door, but yet He had gone.

Then the men thought of all that Jesus had said. "How sweetly He talked to us!" they said; "Did we not feel our hearts burning within while He talked to us!" they said; "Did we not feel our hearts burning within while He was speaking about the Bible, and telling us what it all means?"

Do you think these men went to bed that night? O no! they could not sleep.

"Let us go," they said, "and tell the disciples about our seeing Jesus." So they left the supper, and set out in the night. They walked quickly, and soon came to Jerusalem.

They found the eleven disciples assembled together with some others. They said, "We have seen Jesus, He has walked with us, and talked with us; but we did not know Him till He sat down with us at supper, and broke some bread, and gave thanks to His Father." The disciples said, "Some women have seen Him, and Peter has seen Him."

But while they were eating supper and talking about Jesus, they looked and saw Jesus standing in the middle of the room. Though the door was locked He had come in.

How do you think the disciples felt? They were frightened; they could not believe that it was indeed Jesus Himself.

Jesus spoke kindly to them. "Why are you afraid?" He said. "Look at My hands and feet. It's me." Then Jesus showed His disciples the marks that the nails had made in His hands and feet, and the hole that the spear had made in His side.

The disciples saw that it was their own dear Master. They were very glad to see Him; they had been crying ever since they had lost Him. They saw that He had forgiven them for having run away. He said nothing to them about it; He had even forgiven Peter. He knew that Peter loved Him, and that he was very sorry.

The disciples were so surprised to see Jesus, that they could hardly believe that He was alive. Jesus knew that they did not quite believe; so He said, "Have you anything to eat?" Then the disciples gave Him a piece of fish and some honey from their supper; and Jesus took them and began to eat so that they might see that He was really alive.

Then afterwards He talked to them, and told them why He had died, and that He was going back to His Father to pray for them.

That was a pleasant night for the poor disciples. It was not

like that sad night when Jesus was so sorrowful in the garden.
His sorrows were over, and He never would feel pain any more.

Questions for Lesson 47

On what day did Jesus come out of His grave?
What were two good men doing that evening?
What were they talking about?
Who came and walked with them?
Did they know that Jesus was with them?
What did Jesus talk to them about?
Did Jesus come into the house of the two good men?
When did they find out who He was?
Did Jesus stay in the room?
Did the good men stay in their own house that night?
Where did they go?
Who came into the room though the door was locked?
What did Jesus show to all His disciples?
Were the disciples sure that Jesus was the same Jesus?
What did Jesus eat?

Scripture Verse

How Jesus made his disciples know him again after he was risen.
'...he shewed unto them his hands and his side. Then were the disciples glad, when they saw the Lord.' - (John 20:20).

LESSON 48
THOMAS
John 20:24 to end.

You have heard how the disciples saw Jesus in the evening.

One of the disciples was not there when Jesus came. His name was Thomas. I do not know why he was not there.

When the disciples saw Thomas next, they said to him, "We have seen Jesus. On Sunday night we saw Him. He came into the room as we were sitting together, and He spoke to us. We are sure it was Jesus Himself, because He showed us the marks of the nails in His hands and feet, and the hole in His side where the spear went in."

But Thomas would not believe the disciples. He said, "I do not think you saw Jesus Himself. He died on the cross. I will never believe unless I put my fingers into the marks of the nails, and put my hand into the hole in His side."

It was very wrong of Thomas to speak in this way. He should have remembered that Jesus had promised to be alive again. Jesus heard Thomas speak, though Thomas could not see Him. But Jesus was always with the disciples, and heard all they said, because He is God.

Next Sunday evening the disciples were in a room together. Thomas was there too. The doors were locked to keep the wicked people out; but the disciples knew that Jesus could come in. And He did come. They saw Him standing in the middle of the room. He spoke kindly to them, and said, "Peace to you!"

Then He spoke to Thomas. "Come, here are My hands: put your finger in the marks; and here is the hole in My side, put your hand in it."

Now Thomas knew that Jesus had heard him speak so naughtily, and he felt ashamed and sorry.

He saw it was Jesus Himself, and He cried out, "My Lord, my God!"

Then Jesus said to Thomas, "Now that you have seen, you believe. Blessed are they who have not seen, and yet have believed."

Jesus quite forgave Thomas for what he had said, because Thomas really loved Jesus.

Questions for Lesson 48

Which of the disciples would not believe that Jesus was alive again?

What did Thomas say he must do before he would believe?

When did Thomas see Jesus again?

What did Jesus say to him when He saw him?

Did Thomas believe *then* that Jesus was alive?

Scripture Verse

How God always hears us speak.

'For there is not a word in my tongue, but, lo, O Lord, thou knowest it altogether.' - (Ps. 139:4).

* * * * * * * * * *

LESSON 49
THE DINNER
John 21:1 - 19.

Jesus told His disciples to go a long way into the country, and He said, "I will come and see you again."

So the disciples went away from Jerusalem, and they went into the country. They came to the place where they had once lived by the water-side. They had some ships on the water, and they used to catch fish when they were in the boats.

One night Peter said to the disciples, "I shall go and fish," and the disciples said, "We will go with you." So they got into a ship, and all night long they tried to catch fish, but they could not catch any.

In the morning they were tired and hungry.

They looked up, and saw a man standing near the water-side. They did not know who the man was.

The man called out to them and said, "Children, have you anything to eat?"

The poor disciples said, "No"; for they had caught nothing all night.

The man said, "Let down your net on the right side of the ship, and you shall find some fish."

They did as the man told them, and they caught such a number of fish in the net, that they could hardly lift it out of the water.

Now John found out who the man was: he said to Peter, "It is the Lord."

Peter was very glad, and he jumped into the water, and swam first to Jesus. The other disciples came soon after in their little ship, with their nets and their fish.

Jesus knew that they were tired and hungry. By the water-side there was a fire, and some fish on the fire, and some bread. How kind it was of Jesus to give some food to His poor hungry disciples!

Jesus said to them, "Bring some of the fish that you have caught." So Peter went and took up the net and found it full of great fish; one hundred and fifty-three.

This was a great miracle that Jesus had done.

Then said Jesus to the disciples, "Come and eat." So they all sat down to eat together. Then Jesus took the bread, and gave some to each; and He took the fish, and gave some of it to each.

Now the disciples were quite sure that it was Jesus who was feeding them. This was the way they used to eat together before Jesus had died. Now He was alive, they ate together again; but they knew He was not going to stay long with them.

When they had all finished Jesus said to Peter, "Do you love me?"

Peter said, "Yes, Lord; you know that I love you."

Then Jesus said, "Feed My lambs," (that is, "Teach other people to love Me. Go and tell people about My dying for them.")

You, my little children, are Christ's lambs, and I feed you when I talk to you about Christ. I feed your souls, and the food is the love of Jesus.

Peter did love Jesus, and Jesus knew he did. Yet Jesus said again, "Do you love Me?" Peter said again, "Lord, you know I love you." Then Jesus said, "Feed My sheep."

Jesus asked Peter once more the same thing, "Do you love Me?"

Peter was afraid Jesus did not believe him, and this made him sorry. He said, "Lord, you know everything. You know that I love you."

Jesus said again, "Feed My sheep."

If Peter loved Jesus he would do what Jesus told him, and go and teach people.

Do you love Jesus, children? What would you answer if Jesus said to you, "Do you love Me?" Could you say to Jesus, "Look into my heart, and you will see that I love you?" If you do really love Him, you will hate lies and wrong feelings and you will try to be kind and gentle, and to please Jesus all the day.

Why did Jesus ask Peter so often whether he loved Him? Why did He ask him three times over?

Peter had said he did not know Jesus three times over. So Jesus wanted to hear him say he loved Him three times over.

Then Jesus told Peter what would happen to him when he was old. Jesus said to Peter, "When you were young you walked about where you liked; but when you are old, some men will take you, and stretch out your hands and carry you where you do not like to go."

Jesus meant that Peter would be crucified; men would stretch out his hands on a cross, and nail him there, as they had done Jesus. Wicked people would crucify Peter because he loved Jesus; but Peter would never say again that he did not know Jesus.

Peter was not proud now, as he used to be. And Peter would pray to God to keep him from sin.

Questions for Lesson 49

Did the disciples stay in Jerusalem, or did they go into the country?

Why did they go in boats one night?

Could they catch any fish?

Who spoke to them in the morning?

What did He tell them to do?

Which of the disciples knew first that it was Jesus speaking to them?

Which of them jumped into the water and swam to Jesus?

What did the disciples find ready for them when they were come to Jesus?

Had they caught any fishes in the net?

What question did Jesus ask Peter three times?

What did Jesus want Peter to do if he really loved Him?

How can children show that they really love Jesus?
What did Jesus tell Peter that wicked men would do to Him
one day?
Can you tell me a verse about loving Jesus?

Scripture Verse

Who loves Christ and who does not.
'...If a man love me, he will keep my words......He that loveth
me not keepeth not my sayings...' - (John 14:23,24).

* * * * * * * * * *

LESSON 50
THE ASCENSION

Matt. 28:16 to end; Luke 24:46 to end; Acts 1:4-14.

Jesus used to come and see His disciples after He had come
back to life; but He did not always live with them as He had
once done.

He told them He was soon going up to His Father. "When
I am gone, you must tell people about Me. You must tell the
people who crucified Me that I will forgive them if they are
sorry. The Holy Spirit will come down from heaven, for My
Father has promised to send Him down soon. Wait at
Jerusalem till He comes. I will always be with you though you
do not see Me. Some day I shall come back again."

The disciples asked Jesus when He would come back; but
Jesus would not tell them.

One day Jesus and His disciples walked together to the top
of a hill. Jesus began to pray with His disciples, and He lifted
up His hands and blessed them. While he was doing this, He
was taken up to heaven, and a cloud hid Him at last from the
eyes of His disciples. They still looked up, and saw the cloud

go higher and higher, till they could see it no more. But still they went on looking. Then they heard some persons speaking to them; they looked to see who it was, and they saw two angels standing by them. The angels were dressed in white shining clothes. They said, "Why do you look so long at the sky? Jesus will come again some day." So the disciples went back to Jerusalem, to wait for the Holy Spirit.

Perhaps you think they were very unhappy, now that Jesus had gone. No, they were not. They knew He had gone to get a place in heaven ready for them, and that they would live with Him for ever; and this made them glad.

Questions for Lesson 50

Did Jesus live always with His disciples after He was alive again, or did He only come to see them sometimes?

What did Jesus tell His disciples to do when He had gone back to His Father?

Did He tell them when He would come back?

What was Jesus doing just before He went away in the cloud?

Who spoke to the disciples as they were looking at the cloud?

Were the disciples unhappy when Jesus was gone?

Why were they not unhappy?

Scripture Verse

How Jesus left his disciples, after he had risen from the dead.

'And it came to pass, while he blessed them, he was parted from them, and carried up into heaven.' - (Luke 24:51).

SECTION 10

THIS IS NOT THE END

Introduction
In this section we look at what lies in the future for the world and people who love Jesus, and those who do not.

Some Suggestions for Study
Before each lesson write down one thing that you are excited about in the future. Maybe a birthday present or a holiday or what job you would like in the future. After each lesson pray about what you have written down and then about the better future that is coming when Jesus comes back for those who follow him.

LESSON 51
PETER IN PRISON
Acts 2; 12:1 - 23.

What had Jesus promised to send when He had gone back to His Father?

The Holy Spirit.

And He did send the Holy Spirit, as He had promised. Then the disciples began to speak of Jesus to all the wicked people.

They said to them, "You have crucified the Son of God. He is alive, and has gone up to sit on His Father's throne; but He will forgive you and give you the Holy Spirit."

Some of the wicked people were sorry for what they had done to Jesus, and begged God to forgive them; and some of the wicked people were not sorry, but tried to kill the disciples.

A wicked king cut off the head of James with a sword and then shut up Peter in prison, meaning to kill him soon.

Have you ever see a prison?

It is a dark place, with great doors and bars, and walls all around.

Some soldiers took Peter, and put chains on his hands and chains on his feet, and they locked the door of the prison. Men sat at the door so that no one might get in.

Peter's friends were very unhappy because he was in prison; but they could not take him out. Yet there was one thing they could do; they could pray to God to save Peter, and so they did. Peter's friends sat up at night and prayed to God.

The wicked king said, "To-morrow I shall have Peter killed." But God would not let Peter be killed. So God told one of His beautiful angels to go and let Peter out of the prison. The angel could go into the prison without opening the doors.

It was night when the angel came. Peter was asleep. On each side of him there was a soldier, and Peter was chained to them both. You would not like to sleep in a prison with soldiers near you, and chains on your hands; but Peter knew that God loved him, and that he was safe.

So the angel came. It was dark in the prison.

Could Peter see the angel?

Yes; for the angel was bright like the sun, and made the prison light.

The angel touched Peter on the side, and lifted him up, and the chains fell off Peter's hands.

He told Peter to put on his clothes; and Peter did so. Then he said, "Follow me." So the angel walked first, and Peter followed him. They went through the prison; but the men at the doors did not see Peter go out, for God made them sleep.

Peter was quite surprised; he thought he was dreaming.

At last Peter came to a great iron gate which was locked; but it opened by itself, and Peter and the angel went through.

Now they were in the street. Still the angel went on, and Peter came after him; but they did not speak a word.

All the people were asleep, and did not know that a bright angel was walking in the street. The angel only walked down one street, and then he went back to heaven, and left Peter standing alone in the dark.

Peter stood some time thinking to himself. "What a wonderful thing has happened! I was shut up in prison; but God has sent His angel to let me out. The king meant to kill me to-morrow, but now I shall not be killed."

I know that Peter thanked God for His kindness. He did not stay all night in the street, but went to the house of a good woman he knew and knocked at the door.

Were the people in the house asleep?

No; they were all awake, though it was night.

Why were they not in bed?

This good woman had heard how the king would kill Peter to-morrow; so she and her friends were praying for Peter, and while they were praying they heard a knock; it was a strange thing to hear a knock in the night; but they never guessed who it was.

A maid named Rhoda went to the door, but she was afraid to open it, in case it was some of the wicked people come to kill the poor woman and her friends; so she stopped at the door without opening it, to hear who it was; but when she heard Peter speak, how pleased she was! She knew his voice. She did not say, "Are you Peter?" She was sure it was Peter. She was so surprised that she forgot to open the door; but ran back to her mistress and the rest of the disciples, and said, "Peter is standing before the gate!" but they said, "No, it cannot be Peter; he is shut up in prison."

The maid said, "It is Peter; I am sure it is".

While they were talking, Peter was standing outside, and he went on knocking, because nobody opened the door. Soon his friends ran and opened the door, and when they saw Peter they were quite surprised.

"How did you get out of prison?" they said.

Then Peter made a sign with his hand to make them all quiet, that he might tell them how he got out of prison.

"God sent an angel," said Peter, "who brought me out of the prison. Go and tell all my friends what has happened, for I must go away." So Peter went and hid himself in a place where the wicked king could not find him.

What do you think the soldiers said when they could not find Peter in the morning?

They were frightened; they saw his chains, but not Peter.

They found the gates locked; they could not think how he had got out of prison.

So the king sent for Peter. This was the day when Peter was to be killed. All the wicked people in Jerusalem were expecting to see him. The king's servants said, "Where is Peter? Bring him out."

The soldiers answered, "We don't know where Peter is; he's gone!"

The servants went and told the king that Peter was not in prison. The king was very angry; he said, "Bring the soldiers to me. They must have fallen asleep."

The soldiers could not tell the king how Peter had got away because God had made them fall asleep. The king was in a great rage, and said, "The soldiers must be killed."

What a wicked king this was! He loved to do wicked things. He was very proud, and hated God and God's people. At last, God sent an angel to kill him, and worms ate up his flesh until he died. God sends angels to punish the wicked, and to help people who love Him as Peter did.

Questions for Lesson 51

What did the disciples tell the wicked people in Jerusalem?
Were any of the wicked people who had killed Jesus sorry for their wickedness?
What happened to James?
Where was Peter shut up?
What did Peter's friends do for him when he was in prison?
Who came to Peter one night?
How did Peter get loose from his chains?
How did he get through the great doors?
Where did the angel leave Peter standing alone?
Where did Peter go then?

What were the people in the house doing when Peter knocked?
Why was the maid afraid to open the door?
How did she know at last that it was Peter knocking?
Why did she not open the door?
What did Peter tell all his friends when he had made them quiet?
Where did Peter go then?
Why were the soldiers frightened in the morning?
Why did the wicked king send for Peter?
What did the king desire to be done to the soldiers?
How did God punish this wicked king at last?

Scripture Verse

How the righteous are saved from danger.
'The angel of the Lord encampeth round about them that fear him, and delivereth them.' - (Ps. 34:7).

* * * * * * * * * *

LESSON 52
JOHN
Rev. 1:1 - 19; 4:1 - 5; 22:1 to end.

Almost all the twelve disciples were killed by wicked men at last. When Peter was old, some wicked men crucified him, because he loved Jesus. Now he is in heaven with Jesus, clothed in a white robe, and all his tears wiped away. His dear Lord Jesus is always near him, and this makes him happy.

John lived till he was very, very old indeed. A wicked king caught him, and put him into a country far away from his friends; there was water all round, so that he could not get away.

Was John unhappy there? No; God was with him, and John loved to think of the Father, and of His Son Jesus.

It was Sunday, and John was thinking of God, when he

heard a voice behind him like the noise of a trumpet, very loud indeed. He turned round to see who it was; and who do you think he saw?

The Lord Jesus came down from heaven, all glorious and shining! When John saw Him he could not speak or stand; he was afraid, and he fell down on the ground as if he were dead. But Jesus touched him with His hand and said, "Fear not; I am He that lives and was dead, and look, I am alive for evermore." Then Jesus took John up into heaven, and an angel showed him very beautiful things.

John saw a throne on which God sat. There was a rainbow round the throne. There were a great many seats, and men sitting on them, clothed in white, with crowns of gold on their heads. The men took off their crowns, and threw them down before the throne and praised Jesus, the Lamb of God.

John saw a great many angels, more than he could count, standing round the throne, singing praises to the Lamb.

But of all the things John saw in heaven, there was nothing so glorious as God Himself.

In heaven there is no sun, nor moon, nor candle, nor lamp. Yet it is always light, because God shines more brightly than the sun. The music of harps and sweet singing are always to be heard; for all the angels can sing the praises of God.

John wondered at the things he saw and heard; and he fell down at the feet of the angel who had shown them to him.

But the angel went on speaking, and said, "Jesus will soon come down from heaven to judge the world. He will open the gates of heaven to let in those people who obey God's word; but those who tell lies, and do wicked things, will be shut out."

All people who love Jesus wish Him to come again in the clouds. Do you wish to see Jesus, my little children? Then you may answer, "Even so, come Lord Jesus."

I hope that when you die your spirit will go to Jesus, and that when Jesus comes again, He will bring you with Him.

John wrote down in a book the things he had seen in heaven. All that John wrote is in the Bible. At last John died, and his soul has gone to God. He is with Jesus now in heaven. But when Jesus comes again in the clouds, John will come with Him.[1]

Questions for Lesson 52

Where was John shut up alone?

Who came to see John when he was alone?

What did Jesus show him?

Who did he see sitting round God's throne?

How many angels did he see?

What makes heaven always light?

When John fell down at the angel's feet what did the angel say?

What will Jesus do when He comes again?

Who wrote about heaven and the angels in a book?

Scripture Verse

Christ shall come again.

'Behold, he cometh with clouds; and every eye shall see him, and they also which pierced him...' - (Rev. 1:7).

Notes for Lesson 52

1. 1 Thess. 4:14.

LESSON 53
THE JUDGEMENT DAY
1 Thess. 4:15-17;   Rev. 20:11 to end.

You know that Jesus will come again in the clouds?

Little children, do you know when He will come? You would like to know, but I cannot tell you when; I do not know. The angels do not know what day it will be. No one knows but God.[1] There will be many wicked people in the world then, and some good people.[2] An angel will blow a great trumpet, and Jesus will say to the people who are dead, "Come out of your graves!"

The bodies of all the dead people will come out of their graves.[3] Those who love Christ will be like the angels, and will fly up into the air. If you are alive when Jesus comes, He will catch you up into the air to meet Him.

As soon as you see Jesus you will be like Him, all shining and glorious. Jesus will be king over the whole world, and make all people happy.[4]

At last Jesus will sit upon a white throne, and everybody will stand round His throne. He will open some books, in which He has written down all the naughty things people have done. God has seen all the naughty things you have done. He can see in the dark as well as in the light, and knows all your naughty thoughts. He will read everything out of His books before the angels that stand round. Yet God will forgive some people, because Christ died upon the cross.

Who will He forgive? Those who love Jesus with all their hearts.[5] He has written down their names in another book, called "The Book of Life." He will forgive them their sins, wipe away their tears, and let them live with Him for ever.

Do you hope that Jesus has written down your name in His book?

Ask Him to give you His Holy Spirit. Then you will love Jesus, and hate doing bad things.

This is what God will do to those who do not love Him.[6] God will bind them in chains, and put them in a lake of fire. There they will gnash their teeth, and weep and wail for ever.[7]

God will put Satan in the same place, and all the devils.[8] Satan is the father of the wicked, and he and his children shall be tormented for ever. They shall not have one drop of water to cool their burning tongues.

Many people in hell will say, "How I wish I had listened to the words of my teachers! But I did not listen; and now it is too late. I never can come out of this dreadful place. How foolish I have been! Once God would have heard my prayers, but now I weep and wail in vain."[9]

I hope that none of you will ever speak such sad words.

Remember, Satan goes about as a cunning serpent, trying to make you disobey God; but Christ will keep you from wickedness, if you pray to Him.

One day God will burn up this world we live in. It is dreadful to see a house on fire. Did you ever see one? But how dreadful it will be to see this great world and all the houses and trees burning! The noise will be terrible. The heat will be very great.[10] The wicked will not be able to get away. They will be thrown into the lake of fire.[11] The world will not burn for ever; God will make another world much better than this.[12]

If you are God's child, you will not be frightened when the world is burning; for you will be safe with Jesus, praising Him for having loved and saved you.[13]

Questions for Lesson 53

When will the last day come?
What great noise will there be at the last day?
What will Jesus say to the dead people?
What will be done to the bodies of people who love Jesus?
Where will Jesus sit?
What has Jesus written down in His books?
Whose sins will Jesus forgive?
Where has He written down their names?
Where will God put the wicked?
Who will torment them for ever?

Scripture Verse

The happiness of heaven.
'And God shall wipe away all tears from their eyes; and there shall be no more death, neither sorrow, nor crying; neither shall there be any more pain...' - (Rev. 21:4).

Notes for Lesson 53

[1] Matt. 24:36.   [2] Luke 18:8; Matt. 13:49.
[3] John 5:28,29   [4] Ps. 72.   [5] James 2:5.
[6] 1 Cor. 16:22.   [7] Matt. 22:13. [8] Matt. 25:41.
[9] Prov. 5:11-13.   [10] 2 Pet. 3:10.   [11] 2 Pet. 3:7.
[12] 2 Pet. 3:13.   [13] 2 Thess. 1:6-10.

NOTES

<u>NOTES</u>

<u>NOTES</u>

<u>NOTES</u>

<u>NOTES</u>

<u>NOTES</u>

<u>NOTES</u>

<u>NOTES</u>

<u>NOTES</u>

<u>NOTES</u>

NOTES

<u>NOTES</u>

<u>NOTES</u>

159

<u>NOTES</u>